Colossians

Colossians

The Mystery of Christ in Us

GARY DEMAREST

WORD BOOKS
PUBLISHER
WACO, TEXAS

Colossians: The Mystery of Christ in Us

Copyright © 1979 by Word, Incorporated, Waco, Texas 76703.
ISBN 0–8499–0120–0
Library of Congress catalog card number: 79–63932
Printed in the United States of America

To
Viola Demarest
and
Dr. and Mrs. Louis H. Evans, Sr.
parents in the Lord
who have modeled so beautifully
the mystery of Christ in us

Contents

Preface

For the past sixteen years, as a pastor, I've always taught a weekly Bible class. The discipline of regular study and preparation has literally become my life's blood. The more I teach the Bible, the more its writings fascinate and amaze me. Take, for example, the letters of Paul. How could letters from a converted first-century rabbi to little bands of struggling Christians in a few small towns around the Mediterranean world have any genuine, contemporary significance for us moderns? All I know is that they do!

Recently, I taught the Letter to the Colossians to my regular Bible classes in the La Canada Presbyterian Church and a Lenten study series at the Bel Air Presbyterian Church. The dynamic timelessness of this short letter has gripped me with new force. It's as though a current leader with perceptive insight into the needs and tensions of our time had just written us a letter conveying wisdom and understanding urgently essential for our very survival and meaning.

The letter insists that the clue to the meaning of the universe is: JESUS CHRIST! Why is it so important to focus on Christ? Because in groups of Christian people, peripheral matters have a way of creeping into the center. I've known some people for whom theology and doctrinal matters have become so central that the basic theme of the meaning of Jesus Christ as expressed in his life, death, and resurrection is perilously ignored. Others are known to major in matters pertaining to Christian behavior, insisting that Christian discipleship is basically a matter of behavior often expressed as "no-nos." For still others, the emphasis centers upon various aspects of Christian experience so that feelings and happenings said to be the work of Christ become the ultimate points of reference.

These were the kinds of things that were happening among the Christians of Colossae long ago—but more important—these are the things that still happen in places like La Canada and Bel Air today. And the counsel of the brilliant apostle is as timely now as it was then. I invite you on a journey into one of the great little letters of all time with the hope that it will speak to your condition as it speaks to mine.

Before we begin, let me say a word about the authority of the biblical writings. I'm well aware that this question has been and continues to be a battleground for many, and I have no desire to add fuel to the fire. At the same time, I don't think you should enter into a journey into Scripture without knowing where your guide stands on this basic issue. I stand with those who hold a high view of the authority of the Scriptures. To me, the Bible is unequivocally the word of God. That is to say that in reading the Scriptures I am always addressed by God.

I do not claim any special insights into Paul's

self-consciousness when he wrote, but I do know that when I read his letters I am addressed by God. It has always seemed to me that there are two different ways of stating one's belief in the ultimate authority of Scripture. One is by definition. This might be called the way of the theologian. Here, theories of authority are carefully set forth, and orthodoxy is defined in terms of adherence to the established hypotheses. I have no need to quarrel with this method as it is certainly the most common in the history of theology.

But I have arrived at the same basic position with regard to the authority of the writings of the Bible as the word of God by a different route. My convictions about the uniqueness and reliability of Scripture have been shaped by more than twenty-five years of personal study, application, and teaching. I can only say that I have found the Scriptures to be absolutely reliable and true. Argue if you must, one way or the other, but all I can do is to share my witness of what I have discovered and experienced. I share a common feeling with J. B. Phillips who, after thirty years, based his conviction of the authority of Scripture upon the primary fact that all the way through he discovered them to have a "ring" of truth. I take this reality for my witness, too.

If you have settled for and are comfortable with a particular theory of biblical inspiration or authority, I have no desire to challenge your viewpoint, and I invite you to walk with me and listen to what God is saying to us through his word.

If you are one, however, who has not been able to come to a settled conclusion about the authority of

the Bible, I warmly invite you to join me on our
journey through this little letter, just letting it speak
for itself. Then, you decide whether or not there's
something unique about this ancient writing. If you
hear the word of God, don't be surprised.

Hale Kahu
Hana, Maui
Hawaii
June, 1977

1

What Does a Christian Look Like?

Colossians 1:1–14

As a city, Colossae was a loser. It had been on the skids for a long time and was no longer important. Located about 80 miles east of Ephesus in what is now Turkey, it had once been a city of note. The Greek historian Herodotus, describing the movements of the army of Xerxes, called Colossae "a great city of Phrygia." Another Greek historian referred to it as "a populous city, both wealthy and large."

At one time it had been the hub of the weaving and textile industry of Asia. The wool, clipped from sheep which grazed on the gentle slopes of the Lycus valley, was prized for its superb quality. It was also known for its unique color *collossinus,* the result of an intricate dying process.

By Roman times, Colossae's importance had given way to the two neighboring cities of Laodicea and Hierapolis. You may recall that Laodicea was one of the seven churches of Asia referred to by John in the opening chapters of the Book of Revelation.

Apparently, Paul wrote two letters at the same time: one to Colossae and one to Laodicea. We read in Colossians 4:16 that Paul instructed them to send their letter to Laodicea and in turn told the Laodiceans to share their letter with the Colossians. I've often speculated as to why we have the Colossian letter but not the one written to the Laodiceans. It's rather interesting to note at this point that a massive earthquake was recorded in A.D. 60–61 which leveled the entire Colossae-Laodicea area. The people of Laodicea did a magnificent job of rebuilding and restoring their city, but Colossae was never rebuilt. It seems to me that it is possible in the exchange that Paul's Laodicean letter was buried in the ruins of Colossae and lost to the Christian world.

There's a certain sadness about a town with a great past caught in a period of decline, and that's the way it was in Colossae in the time of Paul. What it was like for the Christians living there then we'll never know, but there is no question that this church was the least significant in terms of location of all the churches to whom Paul wrote. As a matter of fact, unlike Corinth, Rome, Ephesus, Philippi, or Thessalonica, there is no record that Paul ever visited Colossae. Though most everyone else had written off Colossae, Paul honored her with this magnificent letter.

CONFLICT AND CHAOS

The Christians in Colossae were embroiled in bitter controversy. It seems that they were exposed both to the Jewish and Greek cultures and beliefs. For more than two hundred years, Jews had lived in Colossae, and the synagogues were reputed to be lax with tradition and open to all kinds of influences from Hellenistic thought.

Also, this particular area was noted for being the spawning ground for the strange and often bizarre practices growing out of the Greek mystery religions. I've often felt that the spiritual climate of Colossae must have been similar to that in Southern California where I was born and raised, and where I've been a pastor for many years. Our area seems to be a breeding place for any and every cult and fad within and without the Christian tradition.

PAUL'S PLIGHT

As Paul wrote this letter, he was being held in custody by the legal authorities. The traditional view has held that Paul wrote from a prison or confinement in Rome sometime during the last two years of his life. But now, some New Testament scholars believe that this letter was written from some kind of detention in Ephesus during the stormy period of Paul's life which is recorded so vividly in Acts 19 and 20.

Neither view is without problems, but it appeals to me to think of Paul in Ephesus during A.D. 54–57, under some kind of house arrest (as he was later in Rome). By speculating on the possibilities of this setting, it makes the visit by Epaphras from Colossae much more probable, for Colossae was only 80 miles from Ephesus.

This view also places the little letter to Philemon in

this period. It seems much more likely that the runaway slave, whose master was a member of the church in Colossae, had fled to nearby Ephesus seeking the anonymity of a big city, rather than risking a 1,200-mile journey to Rome. Either way, the runaway slave met Paul, was converted to Christ, and sent back to Colossae with Paul's letter asking his master, Onesimus, to receive him now as a brother in Christ.

WHY THE LETTER?

Why did Paul write to the Colossians? The reason seems quite obvious from the content. Evidently, Epaphras had come to Paul from Colossae with grave concerns for the health of the church there. Strange doctrines were being considered and embraced. Apparently, sharp distinctions were drawn between the "super-Christians" who followed strict rules and regulations in certain areas of personal conduct and the "less-spiritual." This led to the kind of bickering that resulted in division and disunity. The culture of the day placed great trust in astrology and horo-scopes, and these practices were being incorporated by some into their belief in Christ. This, too, was a source of controversy. Instead of being united in their faith and practice, the Colossian Christians were at each other's throats.

Apparently, Epaphras felt that only the direct wisdom and counsel of the church's highest ranking apostle could restore any semblance of sanity to the little band of believers caught in conflict. And how powerfully significant that the great Apostle responds with such love and care! Though the little town of Colossae had no significance to the great cities or places of the time, Paul poured out his energy on their behalf and wrote one of his finest letters. We, too, do well to remember that small can be beautiful and that our standards of what is important can be deceptive.

THE CENTRAL THEME OF COLOSSIANS

As we journey through this remarkable letter, three major themes will emerge. The first is: JESUS CHRIST. The universal uniqueness and finality of Jesus Christ is set forth in this epistle as in no other. To anyone who wants to know what the Apostle believed about Christ, Colossians is the best place to begin.

The second major theme is: FREEDOM AND JOY IN CHRIST. Paul vividly portrays the Christian life-style as a bold blend of freedom and joy. There is no place here for a dour, life-denying legalism. The life in Christ is no mere drudgery majoring upon the keeping of religious rules.

The third major thrust is: THE MARKS OF TRUE AND FALSE LEADERS. Just as there were false and true prophets and priests throughout Israel's history, so there are false and true leaders in and among the Christian community. Not everyone who claims credentials as a leader in the church is necessarily to be followed or trusted. Paul was not at all timid in exposing the false teachers at Colossae.

Now, let's begin our journey through the letter itself.

PAUL'S GREETING

Paul, an apostle of Christ Jesus by the will of God, and Timothy our brother, to the saints and faithful brethren in Christ at Colossae: Grace to you and peace from God our Father (Col. 1:12).

Sometimes in our hurry to get into the heart of the letter, there is a tendency to rush through the opening greeting as though it had no more meaning than "Dear Sir." But we must pause at Paul's greeting because it is filled with profound meaning. Remember that he is writing to a church that he had not founded and had never visited. He begins with his favorite title: "Paul, an apostle of Christ Jesus." Of his thirteen letters in the New Testament, he uses this title exclusively seven times. In Romans and Titus, he introduces himself as "servant and apostle." In Philippians, he refers to himself as "servant." In Philemon, he presents himself as "prisoner," and in the two Thessalonian letters he uses no title at all.

The designation, "apostle," had significant meaning: "one who is sent on a mission for another." Jesus had chosen twelve of his disciples to be apostles, and so important was the naming of those twelve that he prayed about it all one night (Luke 6:12–16). One of the qualifications of an apostle was to have been personally commissioned by the living Lord. This commissioning, for Paul, took place when the risen Christ appeared to him on the road to Damascus (Acts 9:1–9).

While his Roman citizenship was treasured by Paul, his role as apostle had even greater significance. While you and I cannot lay claim to apostolic commissioning like Paul's, we can know just as surely that we, too, are commissioned by Christ to be about his business. To be in Christ is to be sent on his mission of loving, caring, and healing. Though we cannot call ourselves apostles in the literal sense of Paul, we can affirm that we are "sent ones" into the world in the name of Christ. I find this to be a source of dignity in my own self-image. You and I are important to God. He trusts us as his messengers—his apostles—and that alone makes our lives significant!

Paul's greeting also points to the special nature of his relationship with Timothy. Paul regarded him with deep affection as though he were his own son. In the letters that bear Timothy's name, I get the feeling that Paul regarded him as a virtual extension of his own personality. That's how close they were. Who wouldn't treasure a friendship like that?

I thank God every day for some deep friendships that I cherish. They're grounded in a common bond with Christ. The friend I cherish most is my wife, but I'm thinking right now of a friendship in Christ that I have shared for more than twenty-five years. I had been out of seminary two years and was engaged in a ministry to students at the University of Washington.

When the UCLA football team came to Seattle to play the Huskies, I was particularly interested in watching their All-American linebacker, Donn Moomaw, for I had heard that he had recently become a Christian. The intensity and integrity that he displayed on the gridiron that afternoon brought instant respect, and I felt compelled to go down to the locker room after the game to express my affirmation.

That casual meeting led to further contact, and a few weeks later, Donn accepted my invitation to come back to Seattle to speak at a weekend conference for our collegians. Something clicked between us, and from that day to this our friendship is one of the most important parts of my life. I know that I can count on his love and support at any time, and I know he feels the same about me. To be sure, we have a lot of personal traits that draw us together naturally. For the past fourteen years, we have been pastors in neighboring communities, and our churches share in some joint programs. But the real source of our friendship has always had its roots in our common love for Jesus Christ.

I find it interesting sometimes among acquaintances in a social setting to raise the question, "Who could you call for help at three in the morning without any fear of rejection?" It's always sad to hear someone say they cannot name any such friend. I'm convinced that friendships grounded in Christ's love can come as close to unconditional love as is humanly possible. Such was the relationship, I'm sure, of Paul and his young friend Timothy.

Paul's greeting in these first two verses was directed

to the Colossians as God's *hagioi*, meaning literally, "God's holy ones."

I'm convinced that most of us, in all honesty, have little desire to be called either "holy" or "saints." But in the language of the Bible, "holy" means to be set apart for the service of God. A vessel in the Temple, such as a chalice, was regarded as holy, not because it had any special virtue in itself, but simply because it had been set apart for special use. We follow a similar pattern. For example, I wear a ring on my left hand. I also wear one on my right hand. The turquoise ring on my right hand cost far more than the simple gold band on my left. But the band on my left hand has far more real value to me because it was placed there by my wife on our wedding day. Though it has little monetary value, it was "set apart" that day for very special use, and in the deepest sense it is "holy" to me. Similarly, you and I are very special to God. We have been set apart for his love and service in and through Jesus Christ. We are "saints" whether or not we like the word. And, hopefully, we can celebrate the word as a mark of distinction.

Paul always links *hagioi* with a geographical location. "To the saints in Colossae." Here is a striking reference to the dual citizenship of the people of God. We are not lifted out of this world for special service to God; rather, we are placed in the world in a given time and place to be engaged in his service. We are called to live in the real world—in Colossae, in Rome, in Los Angeles, or Kansas City—not to escape it or withdraw from it. Each of us in Christ has two citizenships: one in the city of God and the other in the city where God has placed us now. We live out our citizenship in the kingdom of God best when we live with integrity and love in the cities where we are.

Paul concludes his greeting by following an ancient custom in letter writing, adding the salutation of "grace and peace." While this was a customary greeting, these two words had very special meaning to Paul and his readers. Grace means simply that God does for us what we cannot do for ourselves. He accepts us, he loves us, he forgives us, he brings us into intimacy with himself. Peace goes hand in hand with grace. To receive God's grace is to experience his peace.

I see it again and again as a pastor. In recent years, we've developed in our church a special program for people with alcohol-related problems. As a supplement to Alcoholics Anonymous, Al-Anon, and other programs, we've formed a fellowship for alcoholics and their families that focuses specifically upon our relationships with one another in Christ.

I first met my friend, whom I'll call Ted, more than ten years ago. His story was like many I'd heard before. For more than twenty years, he'd been struggling with the disease of alcoholism. Two marriages, five jobs, and thousands of dollars later, he was still under its power. Though he'd tried A.A. before, he agreed to try it again. This time he became a recovering alcoholic and has now celebrated more than ten birthdays of his sobriety.

But after his eighth birthday, he came to the growing conviction that there was even something greater than sobriety. Through prayer and the support of some caring Christians, Ted came to know more of the grace and peace of Christ. He came to experience the assurance of God's complete forgiveness for all of the sins and hurts of the past. He discovered the power of Christ to accept himself in a new way, knowing that God loved him not just because he was sober but because he was a child of God's grace. He has found complete acceptance by God and by his Christian friends—and he even knows that if he were to fail again that he would still be loved. Sometimes when I'm a little edgy or down, I get together with Ted because the sense of God's grace and peace flows through him. Ted is now one of our trained lay counselors, and what a ministry he has to others!

To know God's grace is to be at peace within. To know that nothing can separate us from God's love is the sure ground of inner peace. Grace and peace. . . .

WHEN THE CHURCH LOOKS LIKE THE CHURCH

We always thank God, the Father of our Lord Jesus Christ, when we pray for you, because we have heard of your faith in Christ Jesus and of the love which you have for all the saints, because of the hope laid up for you in heaven. Of this you have heard before in the word of the truth, the gospel which has come to you, as indeed in the whole world it is bearing fruit and growing—so among yourselves, from the day you heard and understood the grace of God in truth, as you learned it from Epaphras our beloved fellow servant. He is a faithful minister of Christ on our behalf and has made known to us your love in the Spirit (Col. 1:3–8).

Though Paul had never been to Colossae, he was happy with the positive side of the report that Epaphras brought him about their faith, love, and hope. Epaphras's report was good news and bad news, and Paul began with the good news. Though most of Paul's letters contained some sharp rebuke and admonition to his readers, Paul customarily began with a strong word of affirmation.

We mustn't miss a basic principle here. It is always constructive, and sometimes disarming, to begin a conversation or communication by affirming the person in some way. My wife, Marily, and I have always found this to be extremely helpful in our relationship with our children. Even when we are dealing with disciplinary matters, we find that if we begin by affirming what we can honestly affirm, it sets a different tone and climate for what follows.

As a member of a local school board, I often receive calls from irate people venting their wrath about something they feel to be wrong with the schools. When I can affirm them for their interest and concern as well as their willingness to express it, I find again and again that the whole tone of the conversation changes. I'm convinced that there's rarely a situation so bad that we can't find something positive to affirm.

In his affirmation of the Colossians, Paul uses his favorite triad of faith, hope, and love. It's found also in Romans 5:1–5; 1 Corinthians 13:13; Galatians 5:5–6; Ephesians 4:1–6; 1 Thessalonians 1:3 and 5:8. The same phrase was also used by the writer of Hebrews in 6:10–12 and 10:22–24, as well as in 1 Peter 1:3–8 and 1:21–22. I'm convinced that these three characteristics were regarded from the start as the true marks of the Christian community, the church. The church looks most like the church when these three qualities are visible. Every pastor and church board does well to ask itself repeatedly, "To what extent is the life of our congregation evidencing faith, hope, and love?" And I think this is a question we should ask about our family as well. Actually, if we have these three, we really have it all.

Faith. *Faith* in the New Testament is a word that involves both the mind and the will. Faith must be grounded in the sufficiency of the evidence. In this sense, it is always rational. To say that we must have faith because we can't understand is misleading and contradictory. One of the men active in our church, attended for many years before professing his faith in Christ. In conversation after conversation he shared with me his intellectual struggles with the gospel. The major obstacle to his faith was the resurrection of Christ from the dead. He hung in there, studying the New Testament, weighing the options and alternatives, investigating, questioning. I'll never forget the day he told me that he was intellectually at home with the witnesses of the New Testament. Only when he was satisfied with the sufficiency of the evidence could he begin to live out the demands of the gospel.

Faith is also a word of action. It means staking my

life and basing my actions upon the object of my faith.
I'm sitting in a chair as I write these words. Obviously,
I have faith in the chair, but my faith had no meaning
until I actually placed my body on the seat. The
validity of my faith does not depend upon me but
upon the chair. My action is based upon my faith, but
the results of my faith depend upon the reliability of
the object. This is an important truth. So often people
try so hard to have a "strong faith." How futile! The
validity of our faith rests upon God's faithfulness, not
upon our capacity for it.

One of my close friends flies his own plane. He is
most gracious in offering me transportation from
time to time. When he first invited me to fly with him,
I had to be satisfied in my mind that both he and his
plane were competent and trustworthy. But even
when I was satisfied with the evidence, nothing
happened until I committed my body to him and the
plane. And my faith has little to do with the results.
My faith is in him and his plane, and the outcome is
totally dependent upon his competency and the
plane's reliability. So far, my faith has been amply
rewarded many times.

The danger at this point is that we approach the
gospel primarily with the question, "Does it work?"
While that may be the right question to ask before
boarding the airplane, it's not the ultimate question
about the gospel. The question of the gospel is, "Is it
true?" I'm afraid that we spend too much effort
trying to convince people that the gospel will get
results. But the issue, as Pilate discovered, is truth. All
of the questions about God, Christ, and the Bible

must be settled in our minds on the grounds of truth. Only that which is true is worth trusting.

Love. The second word in Paul's triad is *love,* the most misused word in our vocabulary. "What the world needs now is love, sweet love. That's the only thing that there's ple-e-enty of . . . " And we croon our love for everything from vanilla ice cream to clothing to sex. Frankly, I don't think we're going to rescue the word, but I do think we need to clarify its meaning in our Christian vocabulary.

Love in the New Testament is not a natural faculty that we exercise. It is a gift given to us by God for relationships. When Paul listed the fruits of the Spirit, he began with love (Gal. 5:22). Here in Colossians 1:8, Paul indicates that their love was a gift of the Spirit. Faith in Jesus Christ always produces the gift of love in us (1 John 2:9–11; 3:11–18; James 2:14–17). Love has much in common with faith, for it also has two dimensions. To be sure, love is a feeling. But true love is action as well. Nowhere is this more clearly seen than in marriage. We grin at the story of the wife who complained to her husband that he never told her that he loved her. He replied, "I love you! I love you! I love you! I love you! I love you! I love you! I love you! Will that hold you for a week?" The words of love must be expressed in tangible deeds or they quickly lose meaning.

The first two words of Paul's triad, faith and love, go together, and either without action is a travesty. There is no question that "faith without works is dead" (James 2:17). The same is true of love.

Hope. The third word is *hope.* The Colossians had a

great past but no future. But in Christ, all of that changes. No matter how black the future may seem, in Christ there is a bright hope for that which is yet to come. This is not wishful thinking, but it is a hope rooted and grounded in God's love in Jesus Christ and based upon Christ's victory over sin and death. Paul stated our hope entirely upon Christ's resurrection and its meaning for our future (1 Cor. 15:12–19).

Theologian Harvey Cox was once asked whether he was optimistic or pessimistic about the future. "Neither," he replied, "but I'm filled with hope." We must not confuse hope with optimism. Hope is that inner certainty that our future is in God's hands. Hope is a perspective that holds the big view of our destiny. It lifts us out of the despair that often comes from the bruises of daily life. It is a healing for the kind of depression that grips us when we have lost our sense of meaning. Victor Frankl, the Austrian psychiatrist, discovered in Hitler's prison camps that those who could affirm some meaning in their suffering were most likely to survive torture and deprivation. Christ gives us the clues to the meaning of life and history. We have our eternal destiny in him. History is moving to its consummation in his return. In his death and resurrection we are set free from the ultimate tyranny of sin and death. Such a sense of meaning produces a powerful hope within us.

Faith, love, and hope are the marks of an authentic Christian community. When people are experiencing together these three, you can be sure you're in touch with an alive church!

WHEN A CHRISTIAN LOOKS LIKE A CHRISTIAN

And so, from the day we heard of it, we have not ceased to pray for you, asking that you may be filled with the knowledge of his will in all spiritual wisdom and understanding, to lead a life worthy of the Lord, fully pleasing to him, bearing fruit in every good work and increasing in the knowledge of God. May you be strengthened with all power, according to his glorious might, for all endurance and patience with joy, giving thanks to the Father, who has qualified us to share in the inheritance of the saints in light. He has delivered us from the dominion of darkness and transferred us to the kingdom of his beloved Son, in whom we have redemption, the forgiveness of sins (Col. 1:9–14).

You can learn a lot about Paul by the way he prays. Most frequently, he prayed for the well being of others. And when he wrote his prayer for the Colossians, he gave them and us an unforgettable picture of what a Christian can become. In four phrases, Paul has given us cameos of the lifestyle characteristic of the disciple of Christ.

Knowledge. Paul prays that they will have genuine *knowledge of the will of God.* This knowledge must always be guided and controlled by the wisdom and understanding of Christ. It's much too easy for us to confuse knowledge with wisdom. Knowledge to the Christian is never an end in itself. Nor does it center in theoretical or theological speculation. How well I remember periods during my seminary years when I was gaining knowledge of the Bible and theology by leaps and bounds, but was hardly fit to live with. It's possible to become very knowledgeable about God

and the Scriptures and still be far from doing the will
of God in daily deeds and relationships. Years ago,
Theodore Roosevelt had this to say about knowledge:
"Take a man who has stolen a boxcar, give him an
education with knowledge alone—and he'll be able to
steal the whole railroad!"

But the person in Christ strives for knowledge
solely as a means of learning the will of God. That's
why Paul was so insistent upon linking wisdom and
understanding to knowledge. Wisdom directs us in
the application of what we know, the blending of the
theoretical and the practical—something most of us
find very hard to do.

I graduated from the University of California in
civil engineering. My first job was with the city of
Pasadena, California, and I was assigned to design a
new storm drain system for an area plagued with
flooding after every rainfall. I had no difficulty with
the theory of designing the project and felt thor-
oughly professional when I sent the drawings to the
construction department. But my ego was shattered a
few days later when I was confronted by a veteran
superintendent: "So you're the bright boy who
designed this project! Maybe you can tell me how to
build it!" I've never forgotten that there can be a vast
gap between the theoretical and the practical. Christian knowledge can be far removed from reality, if
we're not careful. Wisdom is crucial in order to apply
our knowledge to the actual doing of the will of God.

However, "understanding" is needed along with
"spiritual wisdom," and I believe this refers to the
insight that places things in proper perspective.

Understanding enables us to make valid judgments and to keep things in their right place. We are so prone to regard relatively unimportant things with pressing urgency and then turn right around and pass lightly over something that has long-range significance. At times I've become very upset with myself for making some ridiculous mistake in a wedding or a worship service, yet I can be so casual in telling our sixth-grade daughter that I don't have time to play tetherball with her before supper. Mistakes that embarass me will soon be forgotten, or may even provide years of entertaining recollection at family gatherings. But time not spent with a daughter is lost forever—and I'm certain that the will of God has more to do with the quality of my relationship with persons than with my smooth performance in public.

Quality of Life. Paul's second cameo of the life of the Christian disciple is expressed as *leading a life worthy of the Lord.* This cuts at the very roots of our innate tendencies to selfishness. Christian commitment requires decisions that are consciously shaped by the desire to please God and those we love. Merely acting out of self-interest is not enough. We are called to act for the best interests of others (Phil. 2:3–4) as an expression of our love for Christ. The subtle point, not to be missed, is that such actions will ultimately work for our own well-being. I see this all the time in our marriage. Some of my happiest memories grow out of specific actions that were done primarily out of a desire to bring joy to my wife.

But there is even more than the joy and well-being

that comes from living like this. The Christian life is also productive, "bearing fruit in every good work" (1:10). Creative and productive deeds become a natural product of life in Christ. We have an ever-bearing tree in our backyard that produces lemons year-round. That lemon tree never makes a sound—it just goes quietly about its business of producing fruit without any visible effort. In Galatians 5:22–23, Paul listed nine fruits of the Spirit. I suspect that in referring to these qualities as fruit, he meant that they were to become the normal and natural issue of Christian living. Yet we tend to portray them as the marks of a super-Christian. Love, joy, peace, patience, kindness, goodness, fidelity, humility, and self-control should be as normal to Christians as lemons are to our lemon tree.

The life "worthy of the Lord" is also a life on the growing edge of the knowledge of God. I was asked recently to spend an evening with the college group of our church to "rap" with them on the things that I have found to be most important in my own personal growth in Christ. The first thing that came to mind was a Bible study group in my fraternity house. This group was not only significant in my commitment to Christ, but it instilled within me what has become a lifelong practice of regular Bible study. To "increase in the knowledge of God" requires continuing study of and reflection upon the Scriptures. I can honestly say that after thirty years of regular study of the Bible, I am still on the growing edge of my knowledge and understanding of God.

Power. The third mark of the true believer is *power*.

The power given us by Christ comes in the midst of suffering. There's no suggestion here that being a Christian means escape from hardship or tragedy. What is promised is the strength needed to handle trials and trouble.

Here Paul uses what has become one of my favorite New Testament words: *hupomone.* It is usually translated into English as *endurance, patience, or long-suffering.* Each of these terms expresses part of its meaning, but there is much more. All of these English words emphasize the concept of survival—making it through something. *Hupomone* means that we not only endure the trial or tragedy, but that we convert it into something useful.

Brian Sternberg is one of those people who has made an enduring impression upon my life. As a junior at the University of Washington, he was regarded as the leading contender for the Gold Medal in the 1960 Olympics. But in a split second it was all over. During a routine workout on the trampoline, he lost balance and struck his spine on the metal frame. He was totally paralyzed from the neck down. For months his life hung in the balance. His sheer determination to live was undeniable. Instead of competing in the Olympics that summer, Brian appeared before 700 athletes and coaches at a Fellowship of Christian Athletes Conference in Ashland, Oregon. The strain of the trip and the emotional impact of such an undertaking had caused the doctors to advise against it. But Brian was determined to share his feelings with his fellow athletes. Tears flowed freely in that masculine audience as the

paralyzed competitor sat strapped into his wheel-
chair, using all the strength he could muster to
generate a hoarse whisper. In the four or five
sentences he could utter before sheer exhaustion took
over, he shared his undaunted love for Christ, his
trust in God for the future, and his desire to use this
tragedy for the glory of God.

In the years that have passed, Brian looms large as
one of my all-time hall-of-famers. He lives in constant
pain, with only a little movement possible in his
hands. By sheer discipline and training, he speaks
now with clarity. And he continues in his commitment
to bring strength and hope to others—not in spite
of—but because of his suffering. Brian Sternberg has
not only survived, he has chosen to transform tragedy
into something powerful and beautiful. That's *hupomone*. And that's what the Christian life produces. For
you see, that's precisely what Jesus did with the cross.
He took the ugliest instrument of torture and hate
and used it for the redemption of the world.

Gratitude and Joy. The final mark of the Christian
life is *gratitude and joy*. To be filled with the knowledge
of God's will, to lead a life worthy of the Lord, and to
be strengthened with all power is to live a life that
becomes a stream of joy with gratitude. Our gratitude
is based on three great realities with which Paul closes
his prayer—we have been QUALIFIED for an
inheritance, we have been DELIVERED from the
dominion of darkness, and we have been TRANS-
FERRED into Christ's kingdom. That transfer into
the kingdom has brought us redemption and forgiveness. Let's examine each of these three words to get
the full meaning intended by Paul.

We are to be full to overflowing with gratitude and joy because Jesus Christ has "qualified" us for the new inheritance that is ours in the kingdom of light. Every athlete knows the importance of qualifying. To earn the right to play in the tournament, the golfer must compete successfully in the qualifying rounds prior to the main event. There simply is no way that we can qualify ourselves for citizenship in God's kingdom of light. The story of our lives is one of darkness. The Bible's assessment of our history is that of our stumbling and groping in the darkness. To qualify ourselves for the kingdom of light would require absolute purity on our part. Christ does for us what we cannot do for ourselves. As his gift of love to us, we are qualified to share in the kingdom of light.

By the same token, our new life in Christ is portrayed as a "deliverance" from darkness. There's a strange, gripping power of darkness. I recall one night at a conference center heading out to my cabin without a flashlight. There was no moon and no stars were visible. Groping my way along the path I could not see, I experienced the dominion of darkness. I felt like it had literally wrapped itself around me. This is how the Bible views moral and spiritual darkness. It has us in its grip, under its spell. Jesus Christ comes as our deliverer. His light dispels our darkness as surely as one beam of light can be seen from miles away.

This qualification and deliverance results in a literal "transfer" into Christ's kingdom. We are moved from one kingdom to another. Under Christ's rule and reign we have redemption and forgiveness. To redeem is to possess for one's own use. This brings to mind an experience with trading stamps. I can still taste the glue as we pasted those stamps, page after page, until we had enough books to go to the redemption center to possess the desired object. In redeeming us, Christ takes possession of us for his own use.

And this redemption is grounded in forgiveness. God has every right to condemn us, but he offers us his love and forgiveness in Christ. God is portrayed in the Bible as the one who abundantly pardons. The experience of God's forgiveness inevitably leads us into a style of forgiveness with one another. This is profoundly stated in the Lord's prayer: "forgive us our sins, as we forgive those who sin against us." Forgiveness is the necessary dynamic for every meaningful human relationship. In premarital counseling, I try to make this clear. In the romantic surge of a new marriage there's often an assumption that "our marriage will be different," meaning that there will be little need for forgiveness. I'm convinced that we must start realizing that the growing edge of every relationship is the reality of the need for forgiveness—again and again. The fact that my wife has forgiven me so much so many times is one of the many ties that holds us together.

I would even go further and say that a relationship in which two people are not experiencing forgiveness on a regular basis is superficial. It is when we open ourselves to another in some depth that those things in us which cry out for forgiveness and healing become apparent. I need no forgiveness from the teller at the bank—assuming that I behave with reasonable decorum—because our relationship is functional and superficial. I do need forgiveness again and again from the members of my staff because we have agreed to relate at a much deeper level. I treasure most those relationships that require the regular giving and receiving of forgiveness.

SUMMARY

In these initial steps of our journey through Colossians, Paul has given us a clear picture of what it really means to be a Christian. It means to be one who is set apart for the mission of God in the world. It is to be a part of a fellowship where deep and powerful friendships are formed. It means to be a part of a community of people who live by faith, love, and hope. And it means to be a person who is growing in the knowledge of God's will, who is leading a life worthy of the Lord, who is being strengthened with all power, and who is filled with gratitude and joy, even in suffering. It means that we are those who have been possessed by Christ for his own use and who live in the dynamics of forgiveness. These qualities are not reserved for a special few who discover some hidden, spiritual truths or who experience some special ecstasy. Rather, they are the normal characteristics of every person who loves and trusts Jesus Christ.

POINTS TO PONDER

1. Whom could you call for help at three in the morning without any fear of rejection?

2. In what ways are you different because of the grace and peace of God in Christ?

3. Can you identify some ways in which faith, hope, and love were evident in some relationship this past week?

4. How would you describe or illustrate the difference between knowledge and wisdom?

5. Give an example of an experience in which you have seen a tragedy which has been made into something constructive.

6. Identify one thing for which you have needed forgiveness from someone close to you in recent experience.

2

Something to Sing About

Colossians 1:15–23

He is the image of the invisible God, the first-born of
all creation; for in him all things were created, in heaven
and on earth, visible and invisible, whether thrones or
dominions or principalities or authorities—all things
were created through him and for him. He is before all
things, and in him all things hold together. He is the
head of the body, the church; he is the beginning, the
first-born from the dead, that in everything he might be
pre-eminent. For in him all the fulness of God was
pleased to dwell, and through him to reconcile to himself
all things, whether on earth or in heaven, making peace
by the blood of his cross.

And you, who once were estranged and hostile in
mind, doing evil deeds, he has now reconciled in his
body of flesh by his death, in order to present you holy
and blameless and irreproachable before him, provided
that you continue in the faith, stable and steadfast, not
shifting from the hope of the gospel which you heard,
which has been preached to every creature under
heaven, and of which I, Paul, became a minister.

In Jesus Christ we have been moved from darkness
into light, we have been redeemed from slavery into

freedom, and we are granted forgiveness instead of condemnation. From his great affirmations of what it means to be a Christian, Paul now moves into one of the most exalted portrayals of Christ in all of Scripture.

There is good reason to believe that Paul is using an ancient baptismal hymn for the basis of verses 15–20. If so, we are in direct contact with one of the most basic practices of the early Christian church. Write your own music and sing this exalted passage loudly and joyously! I don't know whether or not you've tried reading Scripture aloud to yourself, but this is one of those passages that needs to be heard in order to feel its magnificent impact. Read it aloud. Feel its power. Digest each phrase and focus upon the majesty of Christ.

Let your imagination take you to a quiet setting beside the Lycus River where it courses through Colossae. Gather there with a little band of Christian disciples. Feel the joy as three of your neighbors, newly embracing Christ as Savior and Lord, present themselves for baptism. As your friends are submersed under the water, you are reminded that in Christ we literally die to the old habits and our basic rebellion to God. Baptism is our burial to the old ways. And then, in a powerful and dramatic moment, your friends literally burst out of the water, a dynamic portrayal of resurrection from the dead to a new quality of life.

(There's little question in my mind that baptism in the early church was most frequently practiced by the riverside or shore, immersing the person under the water. What a powerful symbol of the new life in Christ! Paul expressed this dramatically in Romans 6:4, "We were buried therefore with him by baptism into death, so that as Christ was raised from the dead by the glory of the Father, we too might walk in newness of life.")

But let's turn back to our scene by the river. At that moment of resurrection portrayal when your friends come out of the water, you join hands with your Christian brothers and sisters and with joyous abandon sing, "He is the image of the invisible God, the first-born of all creation; for in him all things were created, in heaven and on earth, visible and invisible, whether thrones or dominions or principalities or authorities—all things were created through him and for him. He is before all things, and in him all things hold together. He is the head of the body, the church; he is the beginning, the first-born from the dead, that in everything he might be pre-eminent. For in him all the fulness of God was pleased to dwell, and through him to reconcile to himself all things, whether on earth or in heaven, making peace by the blood of his cross." Could there be any greater hymn? My guess is that this hymn would have had the kind of place in the hearts of the Colossians that "The Old Rugged Cross" or "How Great Thou Art" has to many of us.

THE COLOSSIAN ERRORS

I've already pointed out that Paul's reason for writing this letter was to deal with false doctrines and practices in Colossae as reported to him by Epaphras. Though Paul had never been there, he wrote with all of the concern and passion that he could have brought to his most intimate friends. While we are only listening "to one end of the telephone conversation," we can reasonably guess that the errors which Paul was confronting in Colossae were rooted in a religio-philosophical view called Gnosticism. The Greek word *gnosis* means knowledge, and Gnosticism was a way of thinking that placed strong emphasis upon knowledge as the way to God. This is best seen in sharp contrast to the Christian gospel which holds that the way to God is through faith in God's self-disclosure in Jesus Christ. Gnosticism abounded in secrets and mysteries; and approaches to religion that offer "secrets" about God or the abundant life have an exotic appeal to potential initiates into the "mysteries."

I think it's important to recognize that while false doctrine must be refuted, it need not be feared. Even false teaching and gross error can have a positive result. If it had not been for the growing influence of Gnosticism in the Colossian church, we would not have received this letter from the pen of Paul.

False teaching and practice is ever present in all times and places. Our age is no exception. Who would have dreamed ten years ago that we would witness in America such an incredible wave of influence from the Eastern and Asian religions? Though denying that it is a religion, Transcendental Meditation (TM) clearly grows out of classic Hinduism—the assigning of a mantra in a religious service in which Hindu phrases are chanted and to which the initiate brings an offering of fresh fruit or flowers is, in fact, a religious act whether the initiate realizes it or not. The Hare Krishna movement with its remarkable appeal to many youth is openly a development of Eastern religion. To those of us accustomed to being a part of the Christian missionary movement to the lands of Hinduism, Zoroastrianism, Islam, Jainism, and Buddhism, it has come as a shock to realize that we are now being evangelized by them.

I don't think, though, that we respond best by becoming combative or defensive. This was not Paul's method in the confrontation with Gnosticism. Note precisely what Paul did to the Gnostic challenge. He presented Christ! Very likely, he had done his homework and had a working knowledge of Gnosticism, but in confronting it, he presented Christ. I'm convinced that the challenges confronting us today in the false doctrines of the Eastern religions—or worse of just out-and-out secular materialism—call for the clearest presentation of the unique majesty, love, and beauty of Christ that we can muster.

Not long ago, I was working in my front yard on a Saturday morning when I was visited by two Jehovah's Witnesses. I don't profess to know a great deal about what they believe, because frankly I have no need to. They opened with their stock questions which led into the subject of whether or not I would be interested in studying the Bible. Now, nothing could warm my heart more than being invited to study the Bible, so I responded affirmatively and assured them that I had been studying the Bible for more than twenty-five years.

As an argumentative climate developed, I felt I had

one of two choices to bring integrity to the conversation. I could either enter into a lengthy argument in which, point by point, we would try to refute each other's positions; or I could try simply to share my witness to Jesus Christ as the all-sufficient Lord and God. I decided on the second approach: "I really don't know a great deal about your beliefs, but I will be happy to learn more if you will let me do one thing. Let me tell you in the next three minutes what Jesus Christ means to me and who I believe him to be, and if you can tell me what I am missing or lacking in him I'll be happy to learn from you."

They excused themselves politely but abruptly, and I've never seen them again. I'm absolutely convinced that the best answer to competing religions or conflicting views is to focus exclusively on who we believe Jesus Christ to be. This surely was the method of Paul to the Colossians. The ultimate test, as far as I'm concerned, for any religion or viewpoint is, "What do you think of Jesus Christ?" John Newton long ago set this theme to poetry:

> "What think ye of Christ?" is the test;
> To try both your state and your scheme;
> You cannot be right in the rest,
> Unless you think rightly of him.

GNOSTICISM THEN AND NOW

That we might understand the power of Paul's use of the ancient baptismal hymn in confronting the

Colossian gnostic error, I think it will help to understand at least three of the major teachings of the Gnosticism of that day—teachings in the areas of creation, Christ, and man.

The Gnostics believed that matter was essentially evil and that only spirit was good. Because matter was regarded as evil, God could in no way be involved in the direct creation of matter. The Gnostics, therefore, developed a system of "emanations" involving a number of intermediate beings and stages between God and the actual creation of matter. The farthest removed emanation from God creates matter, and in reality is hostile to God. So went the sophisticated system of "knowledge." This becomes a very basic issue to biblical thought, for in the Bible God is the author and direct creator of all of life and all of matter.

Far from being merely an ancient question of long ago, this continues to be a contemporary issue. Hinduism, for example, carries through a version of Gnosticism in this regard. To the Hindu, all matter is essentially evil. The Hindu cannot accept the Incarnation—God becoming flesh in Jesus of Nazareth—primarily because of his belief that all matter is evil. Therefore God cannot become flesh, for to do so would be for God to become evil.

On the American scene, Christian Science parts company with biblical Christianity precisely at this point. Going an additional step, the philosophical premise of Mary Baker Eddy was that since God cannot create evil and since matter is evil, matter is therefore illusory. Confronting evil in the world of flesh, Christian Science chooses to deny the reality of evil, maintaining the purity of God by divorcing God from real creation. Only spirit is real.

In the world of the Bible, God is very much the Creator of all that is, including matter. The Bible tackles the problem of evil from within the perspective of man's rebellion, called sin, rather than from the philosophical question of evil as such. Thus, in combating Gnosticism, Paul states strongly the relationship of Jesus Christ to creation.

If you were to grant the Gnostic view of emanations between God and creation, then you have to place Christ somewhere along the line of the intermediate beings between God and creation. The view of the New Testament is unequivocally that Jesus Christ is one and the same with God in creation. In no way can he be numbered among the emanations or intermediaries. There is a profound passage in 1 John 4 which sets the New Testament view in concrete: " . . . every spirit which confesses that Jesus Christ has come in the flesh is of God, and every spirit which does not confess Jesus is not of God" (1 John 4:2,3). Here the line is clearly drawn. In Jesus, God has become true human flesh. This was, of course, untenable to Gnosticism. Matter being evil, there was no way that God could become directly involved in human flesh.

In the Gnostic view, Christ becomes one, but only one, of the steps on the ladder to God. I hope you're aware of the fact that this part of the Gnostic error is in no way relegated to ancient times. I haven't met many people who write Jesus off as a bad man or as a deceiver. Most people quickly concede that he was one of the great men of all time. Most people I know would agree that the world would be a much better place if only more people would follow his teachings. But that can be a far cry from seeing Jesus as Paul sees him in this passage in Colossians. The contemporary expression of the Gnostic error is to think in terms of "Christ . . . . and." Christ and success. Christ and wealth. Christ and influence. Christ and acceptance. Christ and country. The list can go on and on, but it always makes Christ but one step toward knowing God or finding an abundant life.

We can't deal with the themes of creation and Christ without raising the question of the nature of man. What is human life all about? Who is man? How does a person relate to God? What is the ultimate destiny and meaning of human life? Gnosticism is grounded in the belief that man finds his meaning and relationship to God by working his way up the ladder step by step. This can come by way of knowledge—learning the special "secrets" and the mysteries, finding the formulas for wisdom and the knowledge of God. And, let's face it, this has a lot of appeal even within Christian circles. We need to be constantly on guard lest we make our doctrine of the Holy Spirit into some kind of special "secret" or "mystery" by which a person can discover the true formula for climbing higher on the ladder to God.

The Gnostics also believed that man could approach God by placating the proper astral deities.

Astrology is one of the most ancient of all religious viewpoints, and it's still very much with us today. When one of our daughters casually explains some particular behavior because she's a Gemini, I'm all too aware that the astral deities have a way of hanging on, even in a modern scientific age. From the opening chapters of Genesis, the Bible is in stout opposition to astrology. The creation narratives make it very clear that the sun, moon, and stars have only one function—to give light and to divide the night from the day. The Bible simply will not grant any power to the astral bodies over man.

Man, according to the Bible, is created by God for a direct relationship of intimacy with him. No intermediaries are needed—least of all angels or emanations or astral bodies.

It is against this backdrop that Paul presents his great picture of Christ. I can't emphasize enough the fact that Paul did not proceed to demolish the views of the Gnostics step by step and argument by argument. He confronts the whole mess by painting a magnificent picture of Christ in the language and imagery of the well known baptismal hymn of the early Christian community. It's as though he says to the Colossians in their struggle with the exotic and esoteric false doctrine, "All you need is what you already have. Not more knowledge, or secrets, or mysteries, but Jesus Christ! Not more and deeper religious experiences, but Jesus Christ!" If you truly know Jesus Christ as God and Lord, nothing need unsettle you.

THE HYMN FOR ALL TIME

Against this background, we are now in a position to appreciate the dynamic impact of this magnificent hymn of the early church. It has but one central theme: Jesus Christ is God and Lord! There are various ways to look at the structure of this hymnic passage, the most common being to divide it into three stanzas: verses 15–16, celebrating Christ as the Lord of creation; verses 17–18a, stating his preexistent activity in creation and showing him as the one who holds the universe together; and verses 18b–20, celebrating his triumph in universal history.

Through a personal friendship with Dr. Kenneth Bailey, a brilliant New Testament scholar, I have been encouraged to view this hymn from the standpoint of its having been a "chiasm." This term is taken from the Greek letter Chi which is the form of a capital X. Dr. Bailey, who has spent most of his life in the Middle East as a biblical scholar and professor makes a strong case for the fact that the chiasmic form is common to literature in the Middle East. The chiasmic form means that a passage is inverted so that the opening phrase is repeated at the end, the second phrase is repeated next to the last, and so on. Without making Ken Bailey responsible for my interpretation here, I find the following structure a helpful way to feel the total impact of this magnificent hymn:

(A) He is the image of the invisible God
(B) The first-born of all creation

> (C) In him all things were created in heaven
>   and on earth (visible and invisible,
>   thrones or dominions, principalities or
>   authorities)
>   (D) ALL THINGS WERE CREATED
>   THROUGH HIM AND FOR HIM
> (C') He is before all things and in him all
>   things hold together (He is the head of
>   the body, the church)
> (B') He is the beginning, the first-born from the
>   dead (that in everything he might be preemi-
>   nent)
> (A') In him all the fulness of God was pleased to dwell
>   (D') THROUGH HIM TO RECONCILE TO
>   HIMSELF ALL THINGS
>   (whether on earth or in heaven, making
>   peace by the blood of his cross)

I don't pretend to be an expert on chiasmus, nor do I set this forth as a New Testament scholarly effort, but I hope you'll find it a helpful basis for feeling the power of this passage. Let's look at the four paired phrases in this scheme.

Image—Fulness (A-A'). I see these concepts as a pair which marks the opening and the climax of the hymn. Image, as expressed in the Greek word *eikon*, carries a much stronger meaning than "reflection" or "like-ness." Because photography is one of my favorite hobbies, when I think of an image I think of a portrait. In one sense, Christ is like a good photograph of God. Generally, people do have a vague idea of God, but it is often out of focus. One philosopher spoke of God as "a vague oblong blur." But in Jesus Christ, we have the true picture of God in clear focus.

A clear photograph, however, does not convey the full meaning of *eikon*. As a boy, Bob Feller, pitcher for the Cleveland Indians, was one of my heroes. I made a standing offer to trade any three baseball cards for one of Bob Feller. I had the largest collection of his cards in our school. I certainly knew what he looked like, how he signed his name, and all the statistics of his great career. You can imagine my thrill in getting to know him personally in the early years of the Fellowship of Christian Athletes. Knowing him as a friend is something totally different from collecting his pictures.

Christ is more than a photograph. "In him all the fulness of God was pleased to dwell." To see and know Jesus Christ is to be in touch with God personally. In him, God speaks and relates to us in a human personality. To know Jesus Christ is to know as much of God as can be perceived by any human being, for he is the *eikon* and the fulness of God.

Firstborn—Beginning (B-B'). Here are two beautifully parallel phrases, one referring to creation and the second to resurrection. "The first-born of all creation" does not have a time sense in the original Greek. It is not saying that Christ is the first of many, but rather that he is the source of *all* life. He is the first in the sense that he is the fountainhead from which all life flows. "The first-born from the dead" suggests the meaning of his resurrection from the dead. Paul's classic statement of the meaning of Christ's resurrection is found in 1 Corinthians 15.

Part of his argument is that "in fact Christ has been raised from the dead, the first fruits of those who have fallen asleep" (1 Cor. 15:20). In other words, because Christ rose from the dead, you and I will be raised from the dead. Christ is the source of life in creation. He is the source of life eternal in his resurrection from the dead.

In these two phrases we have the keys both to the source of meaningful life and to our ultimate destiny. We need to remind ourselves daily that Christ indeed is the only source of genuine life. Bombarded as we are by a plethora of messages from without and within, all telling us that the good life comes from more wealth, possessions, power or whatever, it's easy to lose our bearings and get far removed from the true source.

And Christ is also our hope beyond this life. Each of us must die, but most of us give little thought to that reality. Without becoming morose, it's important to deal honestly with the reality of one's own death. I find that the reality of Christ's resurrection gives me a genuine basis for my growing confidence that death is the entry into a new dimension of life with God.

All Things Created—All Things Hold Together (C-C'). The third pair of phrases in our chiasm exalts Christ as both the Creator and the Sustainer of the universe. Take everything you can see and think of in all creation—the seen and the unseen, all the powers and kingdoms in history, all of the earthly and cosmic forces—Jesus Christ is the Creator! But even more, he is the sustaining force that holds the universe together.

I recall wondering when I first learned that the earth was rotating through space at an incredible speed, what kept us all from flying off in all directions. I was comforted to learn of gravity. I've since pondered why it is that things in our world aren't worse than they are. Our capacity for evil and inhumanity has been demonstrated countless times. Our capacity for destroying humanity on earth has long been achieved—and we continue to multiply our weapons—but something holds back those destructive forces. Paul holds that Jesus Christ is that something. As sure as physical gravity holds our planet intact, so Christ is the moral force of gravity that makes civilization possible. And in the midst of all this chaos, is this crazy group of people called the church. We are to be a witness to the cohesive power who sustains the universe. The implications of this little phrase for genuine unity among believers is unmistakable.

Through Him—All Things Created and Reconciled (D-D'). In my approach, the true chiasmic form is broken here, but I see these paired statements as summary statements of the entire hymn, referring both to creation and to reconciliation. Jesus Christ is the one through whom and for whom all of creation exists. He is also the one who has come to reconcile all things to himself through his death on the cross. The difficult question here is that of the extent of this universal reconciliation.

I can't count the number of times I've been in rap sessions with students into the wee hours of the morning wrestling with this question. It takes the form, "If God's love is universal, how can he condemn those who have never heard?" The additional question of how God can reject those who have rejected him is also raised. The theological position called universalism answers both of these questions by applying Christ's reconciliation to all people, whether or not they have heard or accepted the gospel. This view appeals to me emotionally, and it has a ring of logic. But it raises too many other questions about the teaching of Jesus and the Bible to gain my acceptance.

These questions remain and are painful for all who truly care for people without Christ. In the meantime, I can only hold that God's reconciling love in Jesus Christ is meant to include everyone and everything in the vast reaches of God's creation. Genuine conviction and concern mandates us to be a missionary people. That's why it has been said that "the church exists by mission as a fire exists by burning."

Paul's theology is always a theology of the cross, and the ancient hymn is an expression of the centrality of the cross in our understanding of Jesus Christ. It was in his sacrifice on the cross, in the shedding of his blood, that the reconciliation of the world with God becomes a possibility and a reality. Reconciliation has been stated in recent years as a central theme of the gospel, and rightly so. It is important, however, that we not make reconciliation into something that we can achieve by our desires and efforts. We can only proclaim and work for the reconciliation which has its source and its dynamics in the work of Christ on the cross.

Every time I read this hymn aloud, I have a deeper feeling for the wonder and majesty of our cosmic Christ. I find myself feeling that if Paul had not written anything else, this one passage would have been worth his whole life.

AND THE SONG GOES ON (COL. 1:21–23)

"And you . . . " Paul had no interest in writing mere textbooks for scholars to pour over. He always wrote with ordinary people in mind, the "common man," according to the late William Barclay. The theme with which Paul introduced the hymn is not completed. You recall that his statement of what it meant to be a Christian—qualified to share the inheritance, delivered from the dominion of darkness, transferred to the kingdom of his Son—had led to the singing of the baptismal hymn. Now, the hymn concluded, he returns to the central theme of our relationship with the living God in Christ. We have passed from estrangement and hostility to relationship and reconciliation, all through Christ's work on the cross.

Paul is fond of helping us see our life in the total perspective of past, present, and future. Our past was one of separation, rebellion, and active evil. It is a fact of human reality that evil deeds are always the product of separation and rebellion. Separation from God inevitably expresses itself in isolation from human relationships. Isolation gives birth to resentment and hostility. And once hostility has set in, the seeds have been planted for destructive and hurtful behavior. Such is the normal pattern of human conduct, and history certainly verifies this view.

We see this process amply illustrated in broken relationships all around us. The first danger sign in a marriage or any other relationship is that of withdrawal from communication. The mark of isolation is the refusal to share. And once the process of withdrawal has begun, resentment and hostility is but a step away. Unchecked and unresolved, these feelings eventually erupt into behavior that hurts the other person.

To the Christian community Paul is saying: "This is what you were like." I suspect that this was intended as an antidote to that kind of judgmentalism that all too readily invades the Christian community. How easy it is for us to divorce ourselves from that nasty world "out there" as though our own roots were not deeply imbedded in the same soil. This does not imply that every person has participated in active evil to the same extent as all others, but it is to say that we are all made of the same stuff.

In spite of our past, by God's grace in Christ we are having a marvelous present. Paul uses four highly significant words in these verses. We are *reconciled* by Christ's death on the cross. We are *holy*, and as we've seen, that word means not that we are perfect or even better than others, but that we are set apart for special service to God and to others. We are *blameless*, and *irreproachable*, which means that no charge can be brought against us. Here Paul's great development of the theme of justification by grace through faith in

Romans comes to mind. Martin Luther's classic phrase, *simul justus et peccator*, really says it all: I am at the same time acquitted and a sinner. Herein lies the grace and mercy of God.

And we have a glorious future both here and hereafter. Imagine the impact of words like stable, steadfast, and not shifting to these people in the Lycus Valley for whom devastating earthquakes were common. Our future is stable, for in Christ we are built on a solid foundation. Recall Jesus' parable at the conclusion of the Sermon on the Mount (Matt. 7:24–27). To hear his words and obey them is to build one's life on a solid foundation that will weather the inevitable storms of life.

Both the foundation and the structure must be well built with quality materials. The foundation upon which we build is Jesus Christ. He is the rock that will not be shaken. Our faith in him is tied to the Scriptures, the word of God written for us. A faith that trusts even in the midst of doubts is one of the materials with which we build. A love for God and others which stays steady in the shifting winds of our emotions is the mortar that holds us together. A hope that rises above the fluctuating cycles of success and failure resists the erosion of the seasons of life.

Nowhere are we promised immunity from storms, hardship, and struggles. What we are promised is stability, strength, and security in the midst of adversity. This always needs to be said, for all too often the gospel is presented as though it offered some kind of safe passage without harm or suffering. I've been profoundly moved in recent months by the plight of thousands of Christians under Idi Amin's insane rule in Uganda. With the assassination of Bishop Jumamba, a remarkable man in Christ, I'm reminded that Christian discipleship can be the way of suffering, pain, and even death. But through it all there can be a stability, a steadfastness, and an unshakeable commitment to Jesus Christ, for he is God and Lord.

SUMMARY

In this brief but powerful section, Paul has given us a most exalted picture of the unique majesty, love, and power of Christ. Jesus of Nazareth is the cosmic Christ. The best way to confront false doctrine of any kind is to present a clear picture of Jesus Christ. And there is perhaps no portrayal of Christ more clear and concise than the ancient baptismal hymn of the early Christians.

A growing and dynamic faith in Christ enables us to build the lifestyles and relationships which endure the inevitable storms of life.

POINTS TO PONDER

1. If you were baptized as an adult believer, what recollections do you have of your feelings at that time?

2. In your experience, how do you usually deal with what you consider to be false doctrine?

3. How do you respond to the statement: "Christ is the only way to God"?

4. If you were asked by someone who knew nothing about Jesus, to describe him, what would you say?

5. What does it mean to you to be reconciled to God in Christ?

3

Your Ministry:
Choosing to Suffer

Colossians 1:24–2:5

Now I rejoice in my sufferings for your sake, and in
my flesh I complete what is lacking in Christ's afflictions
for the sake of his body, that is, the church, of which I
became a minister according to the divine office which
was given to me for you, to make the word of God fully
known, the mystery hidden for ages and generations but
now made manifest to his saints. To them God chose to
make known how great among the Gentiles are the
riches of the glory of this mystery, which is Christ in you,
the hope of glory. Him we proclaim, warning every man
and teaching every man in all wisdom, that we may
present every man mature in Christ. For this I toil,
striving with all the energy which he mightily inspires
within me.

For I want you to know how greatly I strive for you,
and for those at Laodicea, and for all who have not seen
my face, that their hearts may be encouraged as they are
knit together in love, to have all the riches of assured
understanding and the knowledge of God's mystery, of

Christ, in whom are hid all the treasures of wisdom and knowledge. I say this in order that no one may delude you with beguiling speech. For though I am absent in body, yet I am with you in spirit, rejoicing to see your good order and the firmness of your faith in Christ.

Paul had a delightful way of flowing from one theme into another in his letters. As he concluded the last section, he referred in verse 23 to his ministry to preach the gospel to everybody in the world. Paul was a man with a cosmic vision. He was the kind of man who rose above narrow parochialism and put his arms around the whole world.

There's a real danger that we fall into the trap of regarding ministers as a special class of professionals who are supposed to do the work of the church while the lay people cheer the clergy on (or boo them out of the stadium!) and make the program possible financially. In this model, the big game is on Sunday morning in the church sanctuary—the choir and the pastors play the game and the congregation, hopefully, fills the stands.

But the model we have in the New Testament is essentially different. The big game was going on all of the time, not in a sanctuary, but out in the homes and on the streets, in the marketplace and in the halls of government where real people were living out the realities of daily existence. The players were not just the clergy, but every man and woman, boy and girl in Christ. The clergy, if indeed there were any in our sense of the word, were player-coaches—instructing, leading, preaching, helping—but always very much in the game themselves alongside the other players.

While Paul was obviously a man destined for very special, apostolic leadership in the early church, he never indicated that he was to do the work of ministry while the others cheered him on. While his ministry was unique by virtue of his being the uncommon man he was, he always insisted that his ministry was a model for every believer. In his profoundly moving farewell to the Ephesian elders, knowing that he would never see them again (Acts 19:17–38), he clearly stated that they were always to be about the same ministry that he had been doing there for two years.

What we learn, then, from Paul about his understanding of his own ministry must be applied to our understanding of our own ministry. While the ministry of the great majority of people cannot or need not duplicate that of Paul, each of us is called to ministry as the basic theme of our lives. The whole concept of ordination has been a great hindrance to the New Testament concept of the ministry of every believer. We best overcome this obstacle not by abolishing the clergy but by developing a clear and strong sense of the fact that every person in Christ is a minister called to the service of Jesus Christ in ministry to the needs of others at every level of life.

One of the most rewarding aspects of my pastoral ministry is to see lay people develop their own ministries. We make the distinction between church work and the work of the church. Church work is all that is essential to maintain and expand the essential programs and activities of the church. It is done by clergy and lay persons alike. But when all of the church work is done, much of the work of the church remains to be done: the work of Christian witness in the home and marketplace, the responsibility for moral and ethical influence where business and political decisions are made and the practical needs of caring for the poor, the sick, and the alienated.

I love and admire my friends Ray and Evelyn Hill. Ray is a butcher and Evelyn is a secretary, but together they have discovered a ministry of compassion and healing. During the past few years they have visited regularly the patients in a local hospital for people with respiratory diseases. I've heard again and again from patients and families their deep gratitude for the presence and love of these two ministers of Christ.

Then there's Dorothy Buss, one of those quiet, unsung heroes. On her own, she initiated a ministry to a local convalescent nursing home. She discovered that there were many elderly patients there who seldom had any outside contact whatever. She enlisted some other people in the church to provide transportation, birthday parties, shopping services, and friendly visits. A number of those neglected folks feel loved and cared for—and we've baptized four of them into the faith—because one woman discovered her ministry.

Jack Samuelson represents the American dream come true. Starting with a pickup truck and a box of tools after World War II, Jack and his brother developed a highly successful construction business. From the start Jack was committed to being a responsible steward of his gifts and wealth. In recent

years he has made unusual contributions to Fuller
Theological Seminary as a trustee. Today, there is an
entire block of student apartments and a new
addition to the library because of his creativity and
generosity of his gifts and wealth. I know of no one
more conscientiously committed to ministry.

One person I'll never forget is Hazel Barthalow.
She's a great-grandmother and had never been active
in the church until about seven years ago. When she
joined she made it clear she didn't intend to be a
spectator, and she also declared that just sitting in
meetings wasn't her thing. She started her own little
"business," taking in clothing alterations and orders
for hand-made woven articles. Every dollar she
makes she gives to our Women's Association to be
used for the costs of shipping and mailing clothing
and food to national and overseas missionaries. She's
contributed more than five thousand dollars to the
projects.

Whether you're a meat-cutter, a housewife, a
wealthy businessman, or a retired great-grandmother, there's a ministry uniquely suited to your
gifts and resources.

THE MEANING OF SUFFERING

Paul here reflects upon the meaning of his ministry
in the light of his imprisonment either in Ephesus or
in Rome. It seems likely that he had numerous
detractors who used his imprisonments as a basis for
questioning the validity of his ministry. We must not

ignore the fact that Paul was incarcerated in some of the finest jails in Asia. And this would have raised the question, "What kind of a leader writes his followers from prison?" When he wrote the Philippians from his Roman imprisonment, he pointed out that some were using that fact to undercut his credibility and to add to his hurt (Phil. 1:15–18). His remarkable conclusion to that situation was that he would rejoice that Christ was proclaimed, whatever the motives of his adversaries. Here he says to the Colossians, "I rejoice in my sufferings for your sake."

Instead of asking what kind of a man writes his followers from jail, the question should be, "What kind of a man can say with integrity that he rejoices in suffering?" The answer for Paul clearly began with his sense of ministry. When you really have a strong sense of mission, meaning, and purpose you can endure all kinds of hardship and suffering for the sake of your mission.

As I've worked with athletes and coaches since the inception of the Fellowship of Christian Athletes, I've witnessed this principle again and again. I've never met an athlete who hasn't played with and through pain along the way. When the commitment to the task is strong, men and women can endure incredible hardships in order to achieve their goals. The most demanding and grueling of all athletic events is the Decathlon—two full days of competition in ten events requiring the whole human range of speed, strength, and endurance. I learned long ago from then World Decathlon Champion Rafer Johnson something of the pain and suffering, year upon year, that these men endure in their training and competition, all for the sake of their mission.

It was never more vivid for Rafer than in the 1960 Olympics in Rome. After two days of grueling competition the Gold Medal had come down to the last event, the two-mile run. To beat his nearest competitor, he had to run the distance faster than he ever had. It was long after dark, and it seemed as though every muscle of his body was crying out for rest. He felt overcome with mental and physical anguish. He stood in a dark corner of the tunnel leading onto the track and dropped his head with a feeling of futility. The piercing shout of his coach, Ducky Drake, broke his melancholy: "Lift up your head, Rafer! Champions don't hang their heads in pain!" With that challenge, all of the suffering and sacrifice of four years of preparation for that moment raced through his mind, and through the pain and fatigue he ran the two-mile in a record personal time, won the Gold Medal, and was later named the world's greatest living athlete that year.

The late D.T. Niles, Methodist leader from Ceylon, told the story at a conference in Princeton of his journey from Ceylon to America. His trip began with a two-mile walk from his home to the nearest village where he then got a bus to take him the last seventy-five miles to the airport. Wearing his open-toed sandals, he stubbed his toe badly a few hundred yards from his home. "On any other day," he said with a smile, "I would have gone limping back to my house, treated my bleeding toe, and spent a part of the day getting all of the sympathy I could get from my wife and children." But on this day, he explained, he was on a mission that was very important to him. If he had returned home to treat his toe, he would have missed the bus and the airplane. His sense of the importance of his mission enabled him to continue with and through the pain, "and you know," he quipped, "by the time I got on the bus I had forgotten all about it."

SELF-CAUSED SUFFERING

But what we're talking about here is suffering that relates directly to our specific sense of mission, pain that would hinder the direct accomplishment of clearly worthwhile tasks. Not all suffering comes to us in that form. The suffering that I know all too well is that which is caused by my own stupidity and selfishness. This has little or nothing to do with my meaning and mission in life. It was not the kind of suffering Paul talked about here as a source of his rejoicing. I can't be very joyful about suffering that is a natural result of my own carelessness or callousness. During my junior year in college, two of us decided a clever system to cheat on open-book exams, regularly given in engineering courses. Each of us would do part of the exam and share our work together, thus reducing the work load by one half. Our ingenious scheme came to naught when I had made a glaring mistake in the middle of a complex design problem by transposing some numbers. Since it had been my mistake, my partner and I agreed upon our summons

to Professor Murphy's office that I would take the
blame for copying my friend's paper. Dr. Murphy
was firm in his standards, and I was suspended from
the university for one semester. I was furious, not
with myself, but with him. Overnight, the whole
direction of my life changed from an officer candi-
date in the Marine Corps to a lowly trainee in boot
camp! I swore I would never forgive Professor
Murphy, and my suffering was intensified by my
resentment for him.

After the war, I returned to complete my engineering course, still holding my resentment and hatred. It
was during that time that I came to know Jesus Christ
personally. This new direction in my life brought
significant insights about the effect that this continuing resentment was having upon me. With
Christ's help, I sought out Dr. Murphy and asked for
his forgiveness. He received me as a young brother—
sharing with me that he was a Catholic believer and
that he had often prayed for me. In that moment, my
suffering and resentment were laid to rest, and I
came to see how God indeed works in mysterious
ways.

There can be no rejoicing in the suffering that we
cause ourselves until we have done what we can to
make amends or to restore broken relationships. But
sometimes we cause suffering that simply cannot be
made right. I think of a teen-ager in our community
driving back to school after lunch hour with his girl
friend by his side. A good buddy is driving the other
way . . . a good natured honk of the horn . . . a playful
turn of the steering wheel . . . and suddenly the

sickening tearing of metal and shattering of glass . . . and the unconscious form of a beautiful teen-age girl impaled upon the gear shift of the vintage auto-mobile. Hours later, she's dead, and a young man must live the rest of his days with the self-imposed suffering of what was meant to be a harmless gesture.

So much of the suffering that I see is of our own doing and bears little relationship, if any, to the suffering of which Paul speaks here. Certainly, the life of Christian discipleship will do a great deal to eliminate this kind of suffering by placing us under greater disciplines and higher motivations, but much meaningless suffering will still be a part of our lives.

SUFFERING THAT DEFIES MEANING

There is another kind of suffering, much more complex, which I think of as the suffering in the dark, gray areas of life. This is the suffering that defies all reason or meaning. The little child with leukemia dying a slow and painful death. The 48-year-old father suddenly stricken with a massive coronary, leaving a bereft wife and children in grief and loneliness. The destructive storm descending without warning on the little village leaving 487 people dead in the ruins and hundreds homeless and destitute.

This is the suffering attributed to "acts of God" by the insurance actuaries, though I frankly cringe at the terminology. This suffering can hardly be a cause for rejoicing partly because of the questions it raises about the goodness and the power of God and partly because there just isn't any easy way of assigning meaning to it.

As a pastor, I'm called in to try to help in this kind of suffering, and I'm frank to tell you that I refuse to profess answers that I don't have. More often than not, I find myself weeping with people and seeking with them God's strength to live with those things that we cannot understand and with which we really cannot cope. You'll never convince me that this is the kind of suffering Paul talks about here.

Suffering as Discipline

There is yet a third kind of suffering discussed in the Bible. The writer of the Book of Hebrews calls this the suffering of discipline: " 'My son, do not regard lightly the discipline of the Lord, nor lose courage when you are punished by him. For the Lord disciplines him whom he loves, and chastises every son whom he receives.' It is for discipline that you have to endure. God is treating you as sons; for what son is there whom his father does not discipline? . . . For the moment all discipline seems painful rather than pleasant; later it yields the peaceful fruit of righteousness to those who have been trained by it" (Heb. 12:5–11).

Again, the world of athletics abounds in this kind of suffering—the suffering of training and development. There simply is no way to get in shape for the competition without the pain of practice and training. The Christian life is like that. If we are really going to be equipped for ministry and mission, we will have to endure the suffering of training. But this is not the suffering of which Paul is speaking here. He has long since endured the suffering of his training; he is really running the race and is now suffering as a mature participant.

It would certainly be a careless and heartless thing, though, to tell a grief-stricken wife that her husband's death is part of her training. We may make God into a horribly capricious coach unless we handle this explanation of suffering with great caution.

SUFFERING WITH REJOICING

I can only be comfortable with Paul's statement about rejoicing in suffering by distinguishing the suffering of which he speaks from these other kinds of suffering. I think it's very clear that he is referring only to the suffering that he is experiencing because of his commitment to the mission to which God had called him; he was being held in some kind of detention or imprisonment because of his faithfulness in exercising the apostolic ministry to which he had been commissioned.

The uniqueness of this kind of suffering consists in the fact that it is voluntary. This is precisely what Jesus set forth as a basic condition for Christian discipleship: "If any man would come after me, let him deny himself and take up his cross daily and follow me" (Luke 9:23). This taking up of crosses clearly refers to voluntary suffering. This must not be confused with the popular understanding of "bearing one's crosses." True, there are crosses that come to us totally unsolicited that simply have to be borne. Some of the other types of suffering I have mentioned are crosses that must be carried involuntarily. My teenage friend has no choice but to bear the cross caused by his carelessness at the wheel. The wife who has lost her husband must bear the cross over which she had no control. There is suffering about which we have no choice; but there is also suffering in Christian discipleship which we choose voluntarily. There are many crosses to be taken up which are not required of us.

The greatest example of voluntary suffering is Jesus on the cross. In a recent study of John's Gospel, I've been impressed again with the fact that Jesus moved through the events leading up to his death of his own volition. John especially gives us the picture of one who is very much in charge of his own destiny, even on the cross. He could have run away, he could have bargained his way out of the whole mess. There were all kinds of things he could have done to avoid the cross. But he chose the way of suffering of his own free will.

One of the best known contemporary examples of this kind of voluntary suffering is that of Dietrich Bonhoeffer. Caught in the web of Adolf Hitler's intrigues in Germany in the 1930s and '40s, this German pastor-theologian chose the way of suffering. He understood before Hitler came to power that National Socialism was a brutal program ignoring God and destroying people. When Hitler came to power in 1933, Bonhoeffer abandoned his academic career, chose the life of a pastor, and renounced Hitler publicly. After two years as a pastor in London, he returned to Germany in 1935 where he was forbidden by the Gestapo to preach or speak or enter Berlin. He then formed an illegal church training college in Pomerania designed to train young pastors, who came from all over Germany, how to live a life of genuine Christian discipleship.

As the pressures on him mounted, American friends got him out of Germany in July, 1939, but he soon chose to return to his own land and people. Before leaving the States he wrote to Reinhold Neibuhr: "I shall have no right to participate in the reconstruction of Christian life in Germany after the war if I do not share the trials of this time with my people." He worked diligently with the Confessional Church, refusing to bow to the totalitarian demands of the Nazis, and was arrested and imprisoned by the Gestapo on April 5, 1943. In prisons and concentration camps he constantly sought to minister to the sick and to his fellow prisoners. He so impressed some of his guards that they were willing to smuggle out some of his writings and even apologized for locking the door of his cell at night. In October, 1944, friends made an attempt to free him and take him out of the country, but he refused in order not to endanger the lives of others. He was hanged by special order of Himmler on April 9, 1945, just a few days before the concentration camp at Flossenburg was liberated by the Allies.

He could have lived out the war in London or in

America without valid criticism. He even could have moderated his position against Hitler and National Socialism as many German Christians and clergy did. But he voluntarily chose the way of suffering—the way of the cross. He believed that the suffering of his people was the suffering of God and that he could make no other choice.

The cause of justice on behalf of the victims of injustice is a cause that no one can require of us but presents us with daily crosses that need taking up. The care and feeding of people in hunger is forever a real need in many parts of the world. No one can require that we become involved in sacrificial love and service, but there are countless crosses that need to be picked up in this desperate area of human need. In the community in which I live, it's easier to avoid those crosses than it is to pick them up. The fundamental basis of lifestyle in suburbia has grown out of the desire to avoid as much of the pain and misery of human existence as possible. I'm sure that's why we are much more successful in programs dealing with marriage and family adjustments among ourselves than we are in attempting to encourage people to take up crosses on behalf of the poor, the hungry, and the victims of social injustice and exploitation. When we start taking up those kinds of crosses we will take on suffering voluntarily. But in that kind of suffering we just might discover the same source of joy that was Paul's in his imprisonment.

Let's face it. We generally avoid involvement in the suffering of others because we regard all suffering as something to be avoided at any cost. The reason

Bonhoeffer lived out his faith heroically was rooted in his understanding of the cross of Christ. To him, entering into the suffering of others was the fruit of his commitment to follow Jesus Christ. Rejection for the sake of Christ was regarded by him as the way of discipleship. To Bonhoeffer, the call to life in Christ was a call to die to our attachments to this world.

> Suffering, then, is the badge of the true Christian. The disciple is not above his master. Following Christ means . . . suffering because we have to suffer. That is why Luther reckoned suffering among the marks of the true Church. . . . If we refuse to take up our cross and submit to suffering and rejection at the hands of men, we forfeit our fellowship with Christ and have ceased to follow Him. But if we lose our lives in His service and carry our cross, we shall find our lives again.*

Albert Speer was one of Hitler's right-hand men through the years of the horrors of the Nazi regime. He served a lengthy prison term after World War II, and upon his release wrote his memoirs. I've never been able to forget a statement he made relating to involvement. He said that he was often asked whether or not he knew what was really going on in the holocaust with hundreds of thousands of Jews being imprisoned, tortured, and killed. His answer, "No, I really didn't know . . . because I didn't want to know!" I'm sure that many of us modern-day disciples, living comfortably and well, can say factually that we have

*Bonhoeffer, Dietrich, *The Cost of Discipleship*, (London: SCM Press, 1948), pp. 74–75.

never taken up some of those ugly, heavy crosses that exist in the world because we really didn't know they were there. But I wonder. How much do we not know . . . because we have chosen not to know? I know that it's past time for me to look around and become more sensitive to the suffering of people around me. And it's time to abandon a lot of the securities I hold dear for the sake of Christ.

COMPLETING CHRIST'S AFFLICTIONS

The second phrase that Paul uses to describe his ministry—and ours—is, on the surface, somewhat bewildering. " . . . in my flesh I complete what is lacking in Christ's afflictions for the sake of his body, that is, the church" (Col. 1:24). The obvious question that confronts us is, "In what sense was Christ's suffering incomplete?" One answer, largely rejected by New Testament scholars, is that this phrase means that Paul regarded his sufferings as completing the redemptive work of Christ. This view is untenable since it places Paul in contradiction with himself. Paul makes an emphatic statement of the fact that Christ's work on the cross is the absolute and final word about sin and our forgiveness. So there is no way that the phrase can mean that Christ's suffering was inadequate to complete the work of redemption for the whole world.

The more likely view, to me, is that Paul is alluding to an ancient Jewish belief that, as a prelude to the end of the age, the people of God would be called upon to suffer in special ways. This suffering was regarded in the same way as that of a woman in labor prior to the joyous event of childbirth. It is suggested that Paul took this Jewish concept of the coming of the Messianic age and applied it here to the suffering which the New Israel, the church, must endure prior to the full consummation yet to come in Christ's return.

Paul never regarded his own sufferings as merely those of an isolated individual. As a Jew, he had a strong sense of corporate identity with his people. As a Christian, he carried the same feeling of his identity with the body of Christ. When he wrote to the Corinthians, for example, he said that his affliction was for their comfort and salvation, and that his comfort was theirs as well. This sense of corporate solidarity is very difficult for us in the Western cultural tradition to come by. Ours has been the background of rugged individualism, and the gospel clearly addresses itself to us in highly personal terms. The appeal of Christ is to the individual with warmth and intimacy.

But there is a sense of solidarity in the whole idea of the people of God and the body of Christ that is basically foreign to us. Those of us who rejoice in our freedom to attend 'the church of our choice' are always in danger of identifying more with a particular pastor, or program, or theology, or lifestyle than with the whole body of Christ.

How can we develop this sense of our union with the body of Christ while still experiencing and expressing life as the individuals that we are? To me, there are two metaphors, both used in the New Testament, that I try to keep consciously before me. The first is that of the human body itself. Paul used this in 1 Corinthians 12, confronting the Christians in Corinth with their excessive individualism by which they had become competitive in their quest for spiritual gifts. Isn't it incredible that we can make a contest out of who can get the best and the most spiritual gifts? It's as though we make the Holy Spirit the author of "games" Christians play. Paul tackled that idea by portraying the body of Christ as a human body.

The body in which we live has remarkable diversity with thousands of members and cells, all with unique functions. Malfunction in one part of the body affects the whole body. Though your legs may be in good shape, if you have tennis elbow your whole body is unable to play well. Get your elbow healed, but pull a muscle in your leg, and you still can't function. The point is that the whole body is interdependent. Each member is an individual to be sure, but each member is dependent upon all of the others. "If one member suffers, all suffer together; if one number is honored, all rejoice together. Now you are the body of Christ and individually members of it" (1 Cor. 12:26–27). I believe that the antidote to our destructive and competitive tendencies in the Christian community is to develop a much more comprehensive view of the body of Christ.

The second metaphor is that of the family. We are the family of Christ, and to those of us who have had the privilege of living in strong and healthy families, the experience of solidarity comes naturally. I see in my wife, Marily, a continuing drama of her solidarity with our daughters, and I share it with her. We talk often about the way in which we absorb so many of their hurts and pains. The tension between giving them all of the freedom they need for healthy growth while at the same time sharing powerful and undeniable emotional bonds that began in the union that gave them birth is frequently overwhelming. Because we are a family, the hurts of one become a source of pain for all. The joys of one become a source of joy for all.

Together in joy and in sorrow we are inseparable when we are truly a family. And so it can be in the family of Christ. In recent years, we have witnessed this in our church with people really feeling joys and sorrows in a deep sense of solidarity. At a wedding in which two of our young people, both deeply committed to Christ, shared their marriage vows, I sensed as much joy and emotion in the four hundred people present as in the immediate family itself. At the conclusion of the service, the congregation spontaneously rose to their feet and applauded! One of our younger men, a husband and father, recently died of cancer. In the months of his sickness and dying, literally scores of people sustained him and his family with prayers and presence. Weeks after his death, his wife said: "I've never felt so completely loved and cared for by this big family of ours."

And now our church is in the process of expanding that sense of the family with the whole body of Christ throughout the world. We've become a part of the family of a youth center in a black community nearby. With money and labor, our people worked with them in the construction of expanded facilities and continue fellowship through various programs. We've been blessed by relating with Keith Phillips and the World Impact program in an impoverished area in South Central Los Angeles. A growing number of our men, women, and youth relates regularly with the people there in tutoring, Bible studies, evangelistic outreach, and crisis ministries. And we feel closely related to the Maasai people in Kenya through a project with Denny Grindall in which we financed the building of some windmills which have brought electricity to that remote tribal village.

To identify and involve ourselves with human need and suffering is our clear mandate. We must recognize that wherever people are suffering, God is suffering. When we enter into the suffering of others, we enter into the suffering of God, "completing what is lacking in Christ's afflictions for the sake of his body, the church" (v. 24).

MINISTRY DEFINED

Paul uses two words in verse 25 of this passage that shed special light upon his understanding of the meaning of Christian ministry: "minister" and "divine office." The first word is the Greek *diakonos,* from which we, of course, get our word *deacon.* The emphasis in this word is on service. It is a much broader term than *apostle,* and can certainly be used

to apply to the ministry of *all* Christians. To minister
is to serve, and the Lord himself is our model for
service. One of the most profoundly moving stories to
me in the New Testament is found in John 13. The
disciples arrive in the upper room for the last meal
with their Lord. There is no servant present to wash
the feet of the arriving guests. This would have
caused embarrassment to them, for it was customary
for a host to provide a servant to sponge off their feet
as they removed their sandals upon entering the
house. It certainly must have occurred to Peter or to
John that one of them could have performed the
neglected task. But apparently, everyone present was
too proud to assume the role of a servant, and they
went to the table with the dust of the road still on
their feet. Then came the dramatic moment! Jesus
rose from the table, took the towel and the basin, and
began to wash the feet of his disciples. Peter rightly
responded by saying, "Lord, are you washing my
feet?" He well knew that it was the servant, not the
master who should be washing feet, but earlier, he
had avoided the servant role.

What Jesus did that evening could never be
forgotten. The lesson was clear. If our Lord became a
servant to his disciples, how much more must they
become servants to one another and to the people all
around them. Ministry means servanthood, yet one
measure of success in our culture is to be in the
position of paying others to serve us. Thus the
voluntary element becomes important. In Jesus' case,
he was a servant not of necessity but by choice. My
friend and associate pastor, Bill Cunningham, teaches

me daily by his example the meaning of servanthood.
He is an exceptionally gifted person and an outstand-
ing pastor. Years ago he chose to be an associate
pastor, not out of necessity, but because he felt it was
where he could best serve. I've never known a gifted
man so eager to serve. He is always looking for ways
to be helpful. He shows an eager willingness to spend
hours with someone who is hurting, needing attention, or looking for a job. And he does it all in a way
that makes you feel important and loved. Such a
servant brings grace and dignity to all around him in
the spirit of the true *diakonos.*

The second term "divine office" is a translation of
the Greek word *oikonomia.* Paul used both of these
terms together in 1 Corinthians 4:1, " . . . one should
regard us, as servants [*diakonoi*] of Christ and stewards [*oikonomia*] of the mysteries of God." The
steward was a servant who had been elevated to a
high position of trust in the management of the
affairs of the household. He remained a servant, but
was given very special responsibilities. We, too, are
called to be stewards. This is our "divine office." We
must always remember on the one hand, that we are
servants and not owners. Yet, on the other hand, we
are given special responsibilities in the management
of the daily affairs of the household of God's
kingdom. In other words, God trusts us! We must
always make central the necessity of our faith in
Christ, but let us not neglect the fact of his trust in us.

Taking our managerial responsibilities as stewards
seriously without thinking of ourselves as running the
kingdom is not always easy. I'll never forget when as a

seminary student, I was spouting off at a social occasion about what was wrong with a particular, well-known world Christian leader. A kindly Christian layman in the group graciously took me aside at the close of the evening and said, "Son, I hope you'll learn along the way that God has called you to be in sales, not in management." I've chalked that up as one of the best lessons I was ever taught about the meaning of stewardship!

Paul saw his whole mission as a servant and as a steward in the light of one all-embracing goal: "to make the word of God fully known" (Col. 1:25). Man's greatest need is to hear that word of God, and there can be no higher goal in the life of any person than that of making the word of God known to those around us.

THE MYSTERY MADE KNOWN

To make the word of God fully known is to proclaim "the mystery hidden for ages and generations but now made manifest to his saints . . . which is Christ in you, the hope of glory" (Col. 1:26–27). Paul uses the word "mystery" twice in these two sentences, and it is obvious what he is doing. The Gnostics took great pride in being the custodians of the ultimate religious mysteries. Using their own language, Paul is now going to meet them on their turf and beat them at their own game.

That the whole nature of God, especially in relationship to men and women, had been veiled in mystery down through the centuries of recorded history, no one could dispute. The Gnostics, like all religions, claimed to have found the secrets of the mystery of God. Such a claim always has intriguing appeal to those who would like to know God. Gnosticism developed esoteric initiation rites which have always had great appeal. One entered the brotherhood by being given secret words and rituals which were never to be divulged outside of the cult. I recall the initiation into my fraternity in which we learned a secret Greek phrase and were given a special handshake grip, vowing never to reveal it to anyone outside of the fraternity. I'll never forget the sense of dignity and importance connected with that moment. The initiation rite of Transcendental Meditation climaxes in the reception of one's mantra—a special word, purportedly given only to the initiate, never to be divulged to another human being. The word is claimed to have a special power to its possessor as long as it is kept secret. All such rites have a strange fascination, supposedly enabling one to have special insights granted only to a few.

The mystery that has surrounded God down through the ages, says Paul, has now been made known fully and remains a mystery no longer. The mystery now revealed is "Christ in you." In other words, that for which thoughtful and searching people have always longed, a real relationship with the eternal God, is now present in Jesus Christ. In Jesus Christ, God not only visited this planet, but now the risen Christ takes his dwelling within the person and within his body, the church. Now it is no longer people seeking to relate to God. It is God dwelling within people, individually and corporately. This is the mystery that could only be made known through the life, death, and resurrection of Christ and that is now open and available to everyone. No hidden knowledge or secrets remain, no mysterious rites of initiation are required, no special language or experience is essential—it is simply Christ in you.

Now, I know I'm treading on dangerous ground here, but I feel something must be said about the persistent tendency even among Christians to present the mystery *revealed* as though it were the mystery *concealed*. A great deal of this revolves around our understanding of the Holy Spirit. The baptism of the Holy Spirit is sometimes presented as though it were some special secret understood or experienced by only a few. Some have gone so far as to develop a virtual initiation rite of speaking in tongues as the sign of receiving Spirit baptism. I sat in a meeting not long ago in which the leader was giving each person phrases to mumble in order to speak in tongues along with laying on of hands and intense emotional encouragement. I have no quarrel with the gift of tongues as one of the many gifts of the Spirit set forth by Paul in the New Testament, but I resist making this gift some kind of initiation rite into a supposed mystery. All of the mystery of God is now revealed clearly, and it is: Christ in you!

Now, to put it simply: I am always in need of growth and expansion in my daily walk with Christ. And I certainly wouldn't suggest that I have opened myself to God so completely that there are no new experiences of his love and grace ahead of me. Not at all. But I do feel the need for constant vigilance lest I make the deeper life in Christ into another mystery religion. It's heady stuff to think you have a secret that someone else doesn't know, especially when the secret purports to have come from God. To the man or woman in Christ there are no hidden secrets. The only mystery of ultimate significance was long ago made known in Christ. God actually makes his home within our hearts—Christ in us, the hope of glory!

In the Fall, we lost our "glory," having been created for relationship with God. In Christ, the hope of our final restoration of glory is a reality. This is the mystery revealed.

In the light of this simple and powerful truth, Paul can honestly say that he regards nothing of greater importance than his continuing efforts to proclaim, to warn, and to teach everyone he can in order to help people come into maturity in Jesus Christ. The Greek word translated "striving" in verse 29 is *agon*. Paul literally agonizes and toils with all his energy to fulfill his ministry and stewardship. He gave it all the energy he had, but always with the awareness that it was God who was at work. I've always felt he summed it up best when he said, "work out your own salvation with fear and trembling; for God is at work in you, both to will and to work for his good pleasure" (Phil. 2:12–13). It may be trite, but I've heard it said, "work as though it all depends on you, and pray as though it all depends on God."

Imprinted on the entry arch to the Benedictine monastery high in the mountains of Subiaco, east of

Rome, is the motto, *Ora et Labora.* Pray and work. What better way is there to express that constant tension that must characterize Christian ministry for us all?

PAUL'S APPEAL TO HIS FRIENDS

Having stated the nature and meaning of his ministry, Paul now makes a warm and bold appeal to his unseen friends in Colossae. Let your mind flow through the words in the long sentence comprising 2:1–3. Encouraged . . . knit together in love . . . assured understanding . . . knowledge of God's mystery, of Christ . . . treasures of wisdom and knowledge. This is what Paul earnestly wants for the Colossians and for us all.

He makes it clear that through Epaphras he has learned there are teachers in Colossae who are deluding them with "beguiling speech." This is the form in which most false teaching comes. It is seldom ugly or unreasonable. It is usually attractive and appealing. That's what makes heresy so difficult to identify. When the false teachers are incoherent and irrational, the task is much simpler. But it's the half-truths, the partial truths, and the specious conclusions that call for eternal vigilance.

When the people of God are deeply rooted in Christ, well trained in the Scriptures, and sensitive to false teaching, "good order and firmness of faith in Christ" are the result. "Good order" is a metaphor of troops under attack that do not break ranks. "Firmness of faith" has reference to the kind of trust which cannot be threatened and will not cave in.

Over the years, we've made a strong emphasis in our church upon the centrality of Christ and upon the importance of studying and learning the Bible. As a result, we've seen a lot of people coming alive and growing in their faith. At the same time, I see them exposed to all kinds of doctrines that proliferate abundantly in Southern California. I have great confidence in these people as I have watched them again and again holding their ranks and standing firm in their faith in Christ. I'm convinced that they know what Paul is about to affirm, that having Christ they don't need anything else.

SUMMARY

In these two paragraphs Paul has given us profound insights into the way in which voluntary suffering is an essential part of our life in Christ. To take on suffering for the sake of Christ and experience joy is one of the paradoxes of Christian discipleship. The suffering of people is the suffering of God. We are called to enter that suffering. As servants and stewards we are to proclaim the mystery now made clear: Christ in us. Such ministry develops people who stand strong together, firm in their love, faith, and hope.

POINTS TO PONDER

1. Many churches state in their bulletins the names of their professional staff and then a caption such as: "Ministers: All the Members of the Church." How do you respond to this? How would you describe your ministry?

2. Can you identify with each of the kinds of suffering described? What is causing you the most pain in your present experience? What can you do about it?

3. Can you describe some suffering in your life that has brought you real joy?

4. Can you identify something that you really ought to do that will probably cause you suffering?

5. What is your understanding and experience of the Holy Spirit?

4

Christis All You Need

Colossians 2:6–15

As therefore you received Christ Jesus the Lord, so live in him, rooted and built up in him and established in the faith, just as you were taught, abounding in thanksgiving.

See to it that no one makes a prey of you by philosophy and empty deceit, according to human tradition, according to the elemental spirits of the universe, and not according to Christ. For in him the whole fulness of deity dwells bodily, and you have come to fulness of life in him, who is the head of all rule and authority. In him also you were circumcised with a circumcision made without hands, by putting off the body of flesh in the circumcision of Christ; and you were buried with him in baptism, in which you were also raised with him through faith in the working of God, who raised him from the dead. And you, who were dead in trespasses and the uncircumcision of your flesh, God made alive together with him, having forgiven us all our trespasses, having canceled the bond which stood against us with its legal demands; this he set aside, nailing it to the cross. He

disarmed the principalities and powers and made a
public example of them, triumphing over them in him.

The last time they had been in my study was three
years ago. That was the day before their wedding. Bill
and Sue were then like most couples I see in
pre-marriage counseling. They sat nestled together
on the couch, hands warmly clasped, faces aglow,
confidently serene. They had grown up together in
our church and started going steady during their
senior year in high school. Though they went to
different colleges, their romance flourished. On the
threshold of new careers, they knew that their
marriage was planned in heaven, willed by God, and
bound to be very special. I shared their joy—they
looked like they belonged together.

But now, each sat on the opposite end of the couch.
There was no touching and no glow. Only the dull
gray ashes of a burned out relationship. To Bill, "the
best day we ever had was our wedding day. It's been
all downhill since." To Sue, "I don't know what's
happened to us. He's not at all the man I married. I
might as well talk to a wall!"

I couldn't miss the parallel with Gordon. He came
in to see me recently, asking if I could help him find a
renewed sense of joy in his Christian commitment.
He shared with me the years of wandering and
searching that had preceded his conversion to Christ,
the love and warmth that he felt from the Christians
in the church he started attending, and, finally, the
amazing love and joy felt in his new relationship with
Christ. The first few weeks were the best of his life,

and then the long, downhill slide began—impercep-
tibly at first, but steadily and surely. And now he had
come to me with the hope that we could work it
through together objectively and he could find new
zest in his search for renewal.

Meeting regularly over the next few weeks, we were
able to discover that the beginnings of his spiritual
pilgrimage were quite superficial. He had become fed
up with his previous lifestyle: the glamor of early
business success and the glitter of the "swinging
singles life" had proven to be a thin veneer. The
discovery of a group of people who really cared for
him and who brought a deeper dimension of integrity
to personal relationships had strong appeal. Learning
a whole new vocabulary, studying the Bible and
praying, sharing deep cares and concerns with others
in a climate of trust, all of these new experiences were
like an oasis in the desert for him.

But the more we probed and questioned together,
the more we were surprised to discover that he had
been relating to the people, the lifestyle, the language, and the forms more than to Christ in a
personal way. Once the imperfections of the people
were as apparent as they had been in his previous
circles, and once the new ways of saying and doing
things had become as familiar as the old ways, the
downhill slide only gained momentum. We came to
realize that his life in Christ had been much like the
marriage of our Bill and Sue. You see, they were so in
love with love, so enamored with the new forms and
language of marriage, that the basis of their relationship was in reality quite external and superficial.

Once the imperfections of the other person had
become apparent, and as the realities of living
together and "keeping house" became old hat, it had
been "all downhill since then."

What a vivid parallel of what can happen in the
Christian life. The discoveries of new words and
songs, a dynamic new community of believers, unusual and sometimes exotic religious experiences,
fresh standards and styles of behavior, and a new
sense of meaning and purpose—these things can
produce all of the wonder of leaving the launching
pad on a flight to the moon. But they may or may not
be anchored in the reality of a genuine abiding,
deeply personal relationship with Christ. If not, we
may be able to sustain our spiritual fantasies and
illusions for some time, but eventually reality will take
over. On the other hand, a growing relationship with
Christ on a truly personal basis can thrive, if
necessary, even on the proverbial desert island.

THE NEW LIFE IN CHRIST (COL. 2:6–7)

Paul knows very well that neither their fellowship
nor his affirmations could sustain the Colossians in
the long run. Only a relationship totally centered in
Jesus Christ is adequate to meet the constant pressures and tensions of daily life and thought. His
appeal to them is that they continue to live in Christ
just as they had received him. The word translated
"receive" is one of those composite words in Greek
which has no one English word equivalent. It really

carries the concept of safeguarding and transmitting a tradition. The central tradition—the mystery now revealed—is "Christ in you." The tradition does not center in a particular theology, experience, or life-style. The tradition to be guarded and transmitted is the reality of the indwelling Christ in the individual and in the church.

Now you and I know very well that tradition has come on hard times in recent years. Traditional forms of worship are out, contemporary and innovative worship is in. Traditional theology is under attack; new theologies press for the spotlight. Traditional lifestyles are scorned, and the new freedom becomes the motif. The dominant note of the past decade has been "relevance," and on that note we've justified a wide range of diversity in faith and practice. We've become more concerned with making God relevant to man than we have with making man relevant to God.

I'm not about to say that relevance isn't important. If I'm using language that you don't understand, no matter how relevant I think it is, it will be irrelevant to you. Ideas and concepts must be transmitted in ways that have meaning to the receiver if communication is to take place. But the danger is that in developing language and forms that are relevant, we change the ideas and meaning of what we are trying to communicate. Those of us who have become involved with "relational theology" are in constant danger at this point. In emphasizing the idea that the gospel is involved in the relationships between persons and God and also between persons, I have often stressed one at the expense of the other. There's a subtle tendency, especially in short-term conferences among people who do not live together in the same community, to major on techniques for developing warm, open feelings for each other assuming that in experiencing each other at deeper levels we are experiencing Christ. This is not necessarily true. We may, indeed, experience Christ in a new way in our brother or sister, but we may be developing a dependence upon another person that ultimately removes Christ as the center of our dependency.

The challenge to relational theology is to maintain a healthy balance between the relational and the theological dimensions of our faith. On the one hand, it is essential that I experience a growing, personal relationship with Christ alone. My love for him must be as real in my solitude, and even in my loneliness, as it is in the midst of affirming friends. But on the other hand, in Christ I am now a member of a community called to love and care for one another. I must never substitute my relationship with others for my relationship with Christ, and I must not blur the distinction between them.

As crucial as relevance and relationships are in the communication of the gospel, we must always be aware that we are to safeguard and transmit the unchanging tradition: "Christ in you, the hope of glory." The cultural elements of lifestyles and worship must always be open to change, but the tradition must be unalterably anchored in Jesus Christ.

How can we develop and maintain the essential balance? How can we be sure that our focus is

genuinely upon Christ? Paul gives us three
metaphors, each reflecting a particular aspect of the
kind of maturity in Christ so essential for every
believer.

ROOTED LIKE A TREE

We are to be "rooted and built up in him and
established in the faith" (Col. 2:7). In this metaphor,
we have the picture of a tree, deeply rooted. Jesus
used the agricultural metaphor in the well known
parable of the soils. Only the seed which fell on the
good soil could send down deep roots and produce
fruit (Mark 4:1–20).

In the parable, one kind of soil produced plants
very quickly. It was shallow with a layer of bedrock
just beneath the soil. In it, the seeds germinated
rapidly, but because the roots could not go deep, it
could not endure the hot sun and the winds. This is a
common experience among new disciples. The climate of the new conversion and the joy of newly
experiencing Christ's love gets things going in a
hurry. But unless there is deep rootage through
careful and prayerful study of the Scriptures and
thoughtful nurture, the inevitable tests of discipleship
expose the rootless life for what it is. It just can't take
the heat or the occasional dry spells.

A second type of soil also allowed the plant to get a
good start. But it contained the seeds of numerous
other plants and weeds. While the good plant started
well, it was soon choked out by the others. Jesus

compared weeds to "the cares of the world, and the delight in riches, and the desire for other things." I've seen many people begin their life in Christ with great enthusiasm only to get bogged down under all of the other pressures upon them. Just making a living and planning our finances takes a lot of time and energy. "Keeping up with the Joneses" can place heavy demands upon us. Sometimes our quest for recreation and leisure can become all too consuming. Our roots can go deep only when we simplify our whole way of life. Sometimes this can be done only by eliminating some of the things that require so much of our time and attention. Such was the case with the rich young ruler (Matt. 19:16–24).

To send down deep roots requires the constant cultivation of our openness and receptivity to the gospel. Only good soil can produce the matrix for daily and wholesome growth. And the cultivation never ceases. The weeds have a way of growing back again and again. But once we have deep roots, we are not easily pushed over or threatened.

We had a little peach tree in our back yard that ended up in just the wrong place when we redesigned the yard to provide more play area for the children. Using my nurseryman's definition that a weed is anything growing where you don't want it, we decided to remove it. It was obvious that the tree's root system was too extensive for transplanting, so I decided to cut it down. Lazy man that I am, I chose not to tackle the horrendous job of removing the stump. It was incredibly persistent, and kept growing until I finally removed the stump and the roots. I'm sure that's why Paul used the perfect-participle form of the verb "rooted" here, which carries the sense of being rooted once-and-for-all. It's so important to get those deep roots in Christ established, for once they're in they are not easily removed.

BUILT LIKE A BUILDING

Paul then shifts to the second metaphor: a building as a picture of the life in Christ. In this scene, though, he puts it in the present tense, so that "built up" expresses something that is going on continually. This picture reminds us again of the parable used by Jesus at the conclusion of the Sermon on the Mount (Matt. 7:24–27).

Life is like building a house, only it is never fully completed. Hearing and obeying the words of Christ is compared to building upon a solid foundation, enabling the structure to endure the storms. On the other hand, hearing and not obeying is like building upon the sand—the structure may look sound and even have the same appearance as the building on an adequate foundation, but when the storms come, the lack of adequate foundation becomes apparent.

We added a room onto our house not long ago as a do-it-yourself project with some good friends helping. First, we dug the trenches, built the forms and reinforcing, and poured the foundation. Up went the walls—sills, studs, braces, headers, board by board, finally tied together and enclosed by the roof and stucco. Hardly any of the materials now show, but each piece is integral to the whole.

Life is like that. Each word that we have spoken, though later forgotten, becomes part of the structure of every relationship. Every thoughtful deed becomes another strengthening member of the whole. Careless or hurtful words or deeds weaken us and others. Building well on the foundation of Christ guarantees the stability of life and relationships, no matter how violent the storms.

ESTABLISHED LIKE A CONTRACT

Next, Paul uses one more metaphor. We are to be established in the faith. The picture here is that of a contract which is legally binding. We all live by many contracts. I recently signed a contract with the college of our daughter's choice. I am committed to paying them a sum of money, and they are committed to providing her facilities, faculty, and classes.

Our relationship with Christ is portrayed here as a contract. When referring to God's faithfulness to us, the Bible prefers the word covenant, which really means that God keeps his side of the agreement whether or not we do. In this sense, God's covenant is different from a contract between equals. The covenant of God, coming to us through Abraham, Moses, David, and the prophets, is now signed and sealed in the blood of Jesus Christ. Paul here suggests that through faith in Christ we sign this covenant with

God, knowing that our security rests in his fidelity.
Our goal is to be faithful to our commitment to him.

A LIFE OF GRATITUDE

The life that truly centers in Christ is ultimately
dependent upon nothing but him. Such a life is
rooted like a tree, being built up like a building, and
established like a contract. The natural outflow of
that life is gratitude. For it is always lived in the
awareness that Jesus Christ is the center and the
source of everything.

I'll never forget a Thanksgiving dinner I shared
with a group of American and European Christians
in Kabul, Afghanistan. To that land where Christian
missionaries are not allowed and Christian proclamation to nationals is illegal, these believers had come to
use their skills in medicine, agriculture, and education to minister to the needs of hurting people. They
were not there as evangelists or missionaries, but just
as people who were willing to let God use their
services for his own ends. Just to be there requires
what I consider tremendous sacrifices. They had left
families and friends halfway around the world. They
were living in houses that would be scheduled for
destruction or substantial renovation in our town.
They were regarded with suspicion by government
officials and generally avoided by locals.

The gusto with which they sang the Doxology
around the table bore witness to their gratitude. One
of the doctors who had left a lucrative practice in the

States to perform eye surgery gratis in Kabul expressed overwhelming gratitude to God: "I thank God each day for the privilege of being here in the midst of such need." A young nurse from London beamed, "I couldn't be more grateful, knowing I'm where God wants me to be." I went to bed that night with a new sense of gratitude—not tied to my material and economic abundance, but to the sufficiency of Christ to meet all our needs.

CONFRONTING THE COLOSSIAN HERESY

Up until now in this letter, Paul has confronted the Colossian false teachers indirectly. Now he takes his first straight shot: "See to it that no one makes a prey of you by philosophy and empty deceit, according to human tradition, according to the elemental spirits of the universe, and not according to Christ" (2:8). He will not let the Colossians ignore the fact that there is a real battle going on. When he says, "See that no one makes a prey of you," he means literally, "don't let any one carry you off as a prisoner of war." The false teachers are portrayed as aggressively seeking captives. This is always what false doctrine is about.

Somehow, we've been lulled into the notion that only we are the evangelists. Don't kid yourself. The most intense evangelists I know are the false teachers. And far from offering you genuine freedom, they want to capture you for their cause; which, by the way, has a profound word to us about the meaning of Christian evangelism. We are not called upon to make captives for Christ, we are called upon to offer all people the new freedom in Christ which will be Paul's next theme in this letter (2:16–3:4). Martin Luther was fond of saying, "If you don't believe in the devil, it's because you've never tried to resist him." If you're not aware that there is a spiritual battle going on for the minds and hearts of men and women, you simply aren't in touch with reality.

ELEMENTS OF THE HERESY

The four terms that Paul uses in Colossians 2:8–15 undoubtedly describe the Colossian heresy more completely than any other reference in the letter. *Philosophy* was a term capable of many meanings. It was used widely by the Greeks in their passion for knowledge and wisdom. It was also used within Jewish religion to describe some of the sects that had arisen. Here it seems to be used to emphasize the fact that the false teachers in Colossae were claiming to have mastered the mysteries of God and the universe by their special knowledge.

Paul immediately labels their philosophy as *empty deceit*. He had no need to be diplomatic here, and he calls it as he sees it, an empty and deceptive sham.

The first reason why this philosophy is empty deceit is that it is based solely upon *human tradition*. The transmission of secrets and religious experiences, the essence of Gnosticism, could make no claim to Divine revelation. The gospel that Paul proclaimed was rooted in God's self-disclosure in Jesus Christ.

Paul stated this with brute strength in his letter to the Galatians. He pronounced a veritable curse upon anyone who proclaimed a gospel contrary to what he had initially preached to them (Gal. 1:6–9). Then he made his dramatic claim: "For I would have you know, brethren, that the gospel which was preached by me is not man's gospel. For I did not receive it from man, nor was I taught it, but it came through a revelation of Jesus Christ" (Gal. 1:11–12). The central issue was always that of revelation. Human tradition is man's viewpoint, divine revelation is God's self-disclosure. And there lies the difference between Gnosticism and the gospel.

The issue remains the same today. There is no shortage of human ideas and tradition. Everyone has a theory about the universe, about God, and about the meaning of life. Some are more plausible than others. They can all be stated in tones of authority and confidence. But either God has spoken in Jesus Christ, once and for all, or he hasn't. If he hasn't, then the gospel is one word among many—take your choice. But if he has, then all other views and traditions must be evaluated in the light of God's word, Jesus Christ. In one sense, you have to take the risk of faith whatever view you take. You gamble on Christ as God's word to the world, or you gamble on some other word. I chose to put my faith in Jesus Christ a long time ago, and I'm convinced more than ever that he is the only option that makes sense.

The second reason Paul gave for calling this philosophy empty deceit was the place that it gave to the *elemental spirits of the universe*. This phrase is actually one word in the Greek, *stoicheia,* and it is used also in Colossians 2:20. The basic meaning of the original word is related to a series of things in a row, one following the other. We referred earlier to the Gnostic idea of "emanations," a series of gods and forces, intermediaries between God and people, controlling the lives and destinies of us all. It is likely that the major focus on elemental spirits of the universe was placed upon a series of astral deities, including the sun, the moon, and the stars. Thus, astrology could have been a central tenet of Colossian Gnosticism.

The belief that the stars and the planets in some way shape and control our lives is still very much present even in our scientific age. As a matter of fact, there are reasons to believe that this kind of thing is on the increase—a logical reaction, perhaps, to our misplaced trust in the false gods of science and technology. As it becomes more clear that technological triumph creates as many problems as it solves, many people seem to be turning back to the ancient superstitions of astral deities and demonic forces— the elemental spirits of the universe.

IF YOU HAVE CHRIST, YOU HAVE IT ALL

Any system or philosophy which makes Christ one among others or which limits the power of Christ to sustain us completely can have no place in the thinking of Paul. It simply is "not according to Christ" (2:8). Again and again we see Paul's continuing emphasis upon the centrality and all-sufficiency of Jesus Christ.

Recently, between sets of a tennis game, I was asked what I thought about one of the current meditation and self-understanding programs now sweeping the country. I replied in essence that I was sure the program was helping some people, and that it was not helping—and even hurting—others, but that I was convinced that there was not one constructive thing in the program that has not already been made available in Christ.

This is precisely what I hear Paul saying in verses 9–15. Paul carries us with him by dramatically using two phrases: "IN HIM" and "WITH HIM." I encourage you to underline them in your text—in him (v. 9), in him (v. 10), in him (v. 11), with him (v. 12), with him (v. 12), with him (v. 13), and in him (v. 15).

IN HIM "the whole fulness of deity dwells bodily" (v. 9). In Gnosticism, the astral deities, the spirit forces, and the demonic powers of the universe served as intermediaries between God and the lives of people. In the gospel, God is personally present in Jesus Christ. Christ is not another of all "emanations" nor is he but a part of the big picture. All of God dwells in him. And Paul emphasizes here the reality of the Incarnation. God dwells in his fulness in Jesus Christ bodily; the fulness of God really lived in human form on this planet in Jesus of Nazareth. Now, if we really believe this, we need not fear whatever powers or forces there may be in the universe, for in Jesus Christ we have all of God.

For IN HIM "you have come to fulness of life" (v. 10). Fulness of life corresponds to the fulness of God in Jesus Christ. In other words, if the fulness of God is in Jesus Christ, and Christ is in you, then you have the fulness of God in you. Do you really believe this? Is this true in your own experience? Or are you still placing more energy than you should in trying to find fulness of life in that next trip abroad or that new boat or condominium or whatever? I'm not saying that the trip is necessarily wrong or that the condominium is essentially evil, but I am saying that you will place these things in proper perspective if the fulness of your life is truly in Christ.

A beautiful woman in my office expressed it well. She had come to share her hurt because her husband had left her for another woman. I'll never forget her statement, "It seems as though all our troubles began after we moved into our dream house on the hill." Fortunately, this doesn't happen in all of our dream houses, but for them, all of their hopes for life's fulness had been centered on the struggle to build the house.

The dream couldn't produce what they needed most—personal communion with God and with each other.

IN HIM "you were circumcised with a circumcision made without hands, by putting off the body of flesh in the circumcision of Christ" (v. 11). Here is language that has an entirely different meaning to us than it would have had to the Colossians. To us, the circumcision of the infant male has long since become primarily a medical and sanitary measure. But to the

Colossians, circumcision was a religious act. The Jewish people practiced circumcision. It was the mark of their ethnic and spiritual identity. In the ancient world, one had no difficulty determining among males who was Jewish and who was Greek. That's one reason why the Jewish men did not participate regularly and freely in the Greek games because in their nudity in the gymnasium they were chided for their circumcision. There could be no more indelible mark of identity. The history of the custom was rooted in God's covenant with Abraham (Gen. 17). Down through the centuries, the sign of circumcision was a constant reminder that God had promised Abraham his blessing: a nation, a land, and ultimate redemption.

In Christ, according to Paul, circumcision now takes on a new form. It is made without hands and consists of putting off the body of flesh. What does all this mean? The body of flesh obviously refers to the life before and without Christ. In Christ, this old body is cut off from us and put away, and a new life in a new body begins. Since this statement is made by Paul as an introduction to the theme of the meaning of our baptism, I think we can say that our baptism now becomes the mark of our identity in the same way that circumcision was the mark of identity on the Jewish male.

WITH HIM "you were buried in baptism" (v. 12). The symbolism here is clearly that of baptism by immersion. I have referred to this dramatic symbolism in conjunction with the baptismal hymn in Colossians 1:15–20. One of Paul's classic statements is found in Galatians 2:20: "I have been crucified with Christ; it is no longer I who live, but Christ who lives in me. . . ." To come to Christ is to die to the old ways of thinking and living, and in the fullest sense to be buried with him.

WITH HIM "you were also raised . . . through faith in the working of God . . ." (v. 12). We are raised from the waters of baptism proclaiming our resurrection to the new life in Christ. Elsewhere, Paul could say, "Therefore, if any one is in Christ, he is a new creation; the old has passed away, behold the new has come" (2 Cor. 5:17). How sad that we have often communicated the picture of death but not of life.

I've always chuckled at the story of the street-corner evangelist who reiterated the same theme to his meager audience day after day: "Before I was a Christian, I used to get drunk every night, but now I don't drink. I used to gamble, but I stopped that. I used to chase women, but now I go straight home." On and on the list went until he was interrupted by a question: "And what do you do now?" "I just stand here and shout at you idiots!"

WITH HIM "you, who were dead . . . God made alive" (v. 13). We were dead in our sins, uncircumcised, without God. But God has forgiven us all our trespasses. Note the word *all.* That's the good news. There is no sin too great for God's forgiveness, and no sin too small to qualify. The meaning of God's forgiveness is now set forth in the vivid picture of a bond signifying a huge debt against us being set aside and nailed to the cross. There are differing interpretations as to what this might mean. It certainly doesn't mean that Christ cancelled the Law. He himself made that very clear when he said, "Think not that I have come to abolish the law and the prophets; I have come not to abolish them but to fulfill them. . . . Whoever then relaxes one of the least of these commandments and teaches men so, shall be called least in the kingdom of heaven; but he who does them and teaches them shall be called great in the kingdom of heaven. . . . Unless your righteousness exceeds that of the scribes and Pharisees, you will never enter the kingdom of heaven" (Matt. 5:17–20). No, he certainly did not cancel the Law.

It's difficult to pin down exactly what is meant by the bond which is erased and nailed to the cross. The most common interpretation of the bond (Greek, *cheirographon*) sees it as a list of charges that has been made by God against us and signed by us as an admission of our own guilt. In this view, Christ is portrayed as erasing those charges from the slate and then nailing it to his cross, making it dead and of no effect.

I prefer a different interpretation which relates this bond to an ancient Jewish story. In it an angel keeps two books on every person: one, a book of sins, and the other, a book of good deeds. With this quaint idea in the background, the bond may be regarded as the book of sins compiled by the "elemental spirits" of the Colossian Gnostics. Agreeing to the charges would make one captive to the Gnostic philosophy. The gospel, however, is the good news that Christ erases the whole book of our sins and nails all charges against us to his cross, canceling their claims against us. Here the cross is portrayed as Christ's total victory over "the elemental spirits."

Thus, Paul acclaims our final triumph IN HIM (v. 15). Christ not only disarmed the principalities and powers, he made a public spectacle of them. It was the custom for conquering generals to march into a city parading their captives in chains—the final act of shame for once proud combat troops.

Here Paul completes the imagery with which he began this paragraph in verse 8. He began his appeal to the Colossians, "See to it that no one makes a prey of you. . . . " He is concerned that not one of them be made a part of the parade of captives of the false teachers in Colossae. He closes with the reality that the false teachers and powers have instead been made part of the triumphal procession of the living Christ.

Doesn't this say clearly to us that we need not fear whatever forces or powers there may be in the universe? If, indeed, it should some day be discovered that the sun, moon and stars do have some power over the destiny of people, we need not fear, for they have been brought captive into Christ's triumphal parade. I have no doubt that there is a devil and that the world of the demonic is no mere figment of the imagination, but I will not fear the forces of evil for they have already been put in chains and have been made a public example. The devil is alive, but he's not well. Battles are still going on, but the war has been won.

SUMMARY

This is the message that needs more than ever to be sounded loudly and clearly to the people of our generation. Living under the shadow of nuclear holocaust, witnessing daily humankind's inhumanity and hostility, feeling helpless and hopeless in a world of mass-everything, we are certainly aware that evil is a stark reality which we cannot avoid. But there remains only one message of hope in every age. It is the same message that Paul addressed to the Colossians. The fulness of God is in Jesus Christ. He is the cosmic Lord of the universe. All things are subject to him. To be in him is to be free and secure. To know him is to have life in fulness and to be able to affirm with Paul: "Who shall separate us from the love of Christ? Shall tribulation, or distress, or persecution, or famine, or nakedness, or peril, or sword? . . . No, in all these things we are more than conquerors through him who loved us. For I am sure that neither death, nor life, nor angels, nor principalities, nor things present, nor things to come, nor powers, nor height, nor depth, nor anything else in all creation, will be able to separate us from the love of God in Christ Jesus our Lord" (Rom. 8:35–39).

Points to Ponder

1.   Have you experienced periods of "cooling off" in your relationship with Christ? What causes them? How do you find renewal?

2.   Do you tend to place more emphasis upon doctrine or upon relationships? How do you go about keeping them in healthy tension?

3.   Which metaphor best describes your walk with Christ: the tree, the building, or the contract?

4.   Can you identify any of your feelings or beliefs with those of the Colossian heresy?

5.   List some specific ways in which Christ meets some of your needs.

6.   Can you think of some ways in which some Christians are really suggesting that Christ alone is not enough?

5

Living Beyond the Rules

Colossians 2:16–3:4

Therefore let no one pass judgment on you in questions of food and drink or with regard to a festival or a new moon or a sabbath. These are only a shadow of what is to come but the substance belongs to Christ. Let no one disqualify you, insisting on self-abasement and worship of angels, taking his stand on visions, puffed up without reason by his sensuous mind, and not holding fast to the Head, from whom the whole body, nourished and knit together through its joints and ligaments, grows with a growth that is from God.

If with Christ you died to the elemental spirits of the universe, why do you live as if you still belonged to the world? Why do you submit to regulations, "Do not handle, Do not taste, Do not touch" (referring to things which all perish as they are used), according to human precepts and doctrines? These have indeed an appearance of wisdom in promoting rigor of devotion and self-abasement and severity to the body, but they are of no value in checking the indulgence of the flesh.

If then you have been raised with Christ, seek the

113

things that are above, where Christ is, seated at the right hand of God. Set your minds on things that are above, not on things that are on earth. For you have died, and your life is hid with Christ in God. When Christ who is our life appears, then you also will appear with him in glory.

Paul had no difficulty moving back and forth between the doctrinal and the practical. In earlier verses he has taken us into the depths of our doctrinal understanding of the person and work of Jesus Christ. He has soared high into the heavens of theological insight. And now with one strategic word—THEREFORE—he brings us squarely into the world of the nitty-gritty, everyday decisions about behavior. He has literally demolished the doctrinal and philosophical premises of the Gnostics at Colossae by his clear presentation of Christ, and now he is going to take them to account on the practical applications of their specious beliefs. Paul was well aware of the fact that all beliefs produce certain types of behavior, and all behavior reflects certain beliefs.

There is a great deal of talk these days about moral and spiritual values in public life. And in my opinion this dialogue has begun none too soon, for we have certainly come to a crisis in values throughout national life. The Watergate scandals of the early 1970s are best understood not simply as the misdeeds of a few evil men, but as the natural outcome of an entire generation caught in the throes of moral incertitude.

For many years now there seems to have been a tacit assumption that we could be neutral about moral values, that such things were up to the individual, but we are now realizing that neutrality itself reflects a value system. Values are being taught in our homes, our schools, our business institutions—everywhere, either by precept, example, or even by silence. And without some consensus about such values as honesty, goodness, the rights of others, and the importance of the family, no civilization can long endure.

In the American system, we are committed to the right of every person to hold any or no religious beliefs. The Constitution guarantees that there shall be no official, established religion. But on the other hand, values are the by-product of what we believe about the ultimate meaning of persons, society, and history. The unresolved dilemma of the American way of life is how to achieve the consensus in values essential for the survival of a civilization without an official religious establishment. I don't find any answer to this other than my conviction to live my life in Christ in such a way that the total Christian community of which I am a part will be a positive and a credible force in our time.

It's right here that we can be very forthright about the gospel. There's nothing soft or sterile about it when it comes to clear statements about moral and spiritual values. It doesn't leave us guessing about standards of love and goodness, justice and right-eousness, truth and error, integrity and falsehood. The Bible abounds with enduring principles and specific applications in behavior. Though we may differ in our interpretations, we cannot ignore the clear absolutes and imperatives throughout the Scrip-tures.

The Christian faith is not a theology to be debated

or defended. It is a vigorous and productive life to be lived, centered upon Jesus Christ. Paul affirmed this truth as he consistently kept his theology tightly bound to practice and his conduct tied to doctrine. When he wrote to the Ephesians, for example, he spent the first three chapters talking about doctrine, and then he moved on to an application of the gospel to daily living in the last three chapters. The Apostle also follows the same pattern in the Book of Romans as he presents a brilliant theological discussion in the first eleven chapters. Then his opening "therefore" in chapter twelve introduces a ringing appeal for the practical aspects of Christian living.

In Ephesians, for example, a high and exalted view of Christ is the basis for a meaningful marriage. In Romans, a deep understanding of justification by grace through faith is the foundation for living in harmony within the Christian community. It is this pattern in Paul that reminds us that doctrinal teaching that does not emphasize practice is ultimately worthless. Likewise, ethical teaching that is not grounded in doctrine is innocuous. The other side of the coin, as demonstrated in Colossae, is that false doctrine inevitably produces false practice. In the same way, persistence in false behavior will lead to false doctrine.

FREEDOM FROM THE JUDGMENT OF OTHERS

In verses 16–19, Paul begins his attack on the false practices of the Gnostics by asserting the freedom of the believers from the guilt producing judgmentalism aimed at them. I suspect it went something like this: "If you really are a good Christian, how come you eat lobster and drink wine? It has long been established that we do not do those things." Or, "If you are a good Christian, how come you go to the beach on the Sabbath?" And on and on it goes.

One of the tragic and utterly false notions most of us have is that any discussion of Christian behavior is regulated by a rather rigid list of rules and regulations—do's and don'ts. Now, there's no doubt but that we have to flesh out our standards, but this must not be where we begin.

You see, if we begin with rules, the emphasis will center upon our performance, and when this happens, everything we do and say is triggered by a stiff and unrelenting legalism. But if we begin with an emphasis upon who we are in our relationship with Christ, we will live in a climate of freedom from such judgmentalism. While it is true that freedom can be exploited and abused, this is where we must begin if we are going to be faithful to the approach of Paul.

At least five kinds of behavior were being used to produce guilt feelings among the Colossians. Paul refers to them as food and drink, holy days, false humility, angel worship, and visions. It was over these things that the Christian community was divided, and Paul demands that they cease judging one another over these matters.

Though the lists of issues change in different times and places, the tendency to pick at each other is incredibly persistent. But all such judging violates one cardinal principle: we are justified by God's grace through faith in Jesus Christ. We are judged by God alone, and he declares us "not guilty" in Jesus Christ. While this in no way alleviates our responsibility to one another, it never means that we are to judge each other. We are to live in responsible freedom.

FOOD AND DRINK

This apparently has always been a battleground in all types of religious communities. Rules and regulations about food and drink are ever present, probably because eating and drinking is so essential to life. From Old Testament times, dietary laws were a part of Israel's heritage. Many of those laws were obviously based upon principles of basic health and sanitation, particularly in a culture without refrigeration or modern preservatives. For example, there was an absolute prohibition upon eating the meat of camels, rock badgers, rabbits, and pigs because none of them "parted the hoof and chewed the cud" (Lev. 11:1–8). Neither were they to eat anything out of the waters that did not have fins and scales (Lev. 11:9–12). The ban also applied to eagles, falcons, hawks, sea gulls, owls, water hens, pelicans, bats, and many other birds (Lev. 11:13–19). In addition, all winged insects were forbidden except "those which have legs above their feet, with which to leap on the earth" (Lev. 11:21). Thus locusts, crickets, and grasshoppers were acceptable treats! The list goes on to exclude weasels, mice, lizards, crocodiles, chameleons, and even the lowly gecko, presumably an endangered species who didn't make it (Lev. 11:29–30).

Imagine how difficult it must have been for Paul and other Jewish Christians suddenly to break from centuries of tradition! It sure wasn't easy for Peter. He even argued with God when he was given the vision before his lunch hour of the sheet being lowered with some of these unclean animals and the command to kill and eat (Acts 10:9–23). His freedom from the old dietary laws was his first step toward the greater freedom to accept a Gentile as a brother in Jesus Christ. In his proclamation at the house of Cornelius, Peter made it clear for us all that the old rules as to what was clean and unclean are relegated by Christ to the realm of the trivial (Acts 10:24–43).

Such a radical break from time-honored rules and regulations was likely to produce some all-too-human excesses. It certainly did in Corinth. They apparently had no difficulty abandoning the rules; in fact, they went overboard in their new freedom. They had even gone so far as drinking far too much wine at the Lord's Supper. It has even been implied that the "love feast" often became an orgy. Such excesses were addressed harshly by Paul (1 Cor. 11:17–34) with strong demands that they bring their new freedom under control.

It's not uncommon to become irresponsible in matters of eating and drinking when the bonds of legalism are broken. I've seen it often in people who were raised in homes with oppressive restrictions in such areas. I've also seen it among Christians who came to a new sense of freedom out of a legalistic style. When we are moving away from legalism, with Peter and Paul, we do well to remember the Corinthians! Freedom must always have boundaries. Paul made it so clear: "Only take care lest this liberty of yours somehow become a stumbling block to the weak" (1 Cor. 8:9). "All things are lawful, but not all things are helpful. All things are lawful, but not all things build up. Let no one seek his own good, but the good of his neighbor" (1 Cor. 10:23–24). Concern for our example and influence is the essence of responsible freedom.

In Rome, however, the matter took another twist. To the Colossians the appeal is totally on the side of freedom. To the Corinthians, the admonition is completely toward responsibility. To the Romans, Paul has strong words on both sides. Apparently, the abstainers were judging the indulgers for not being responsible, and the indulgers were blasting the abstainers for not exercising their freedom. I can identify best with the Roman situation for it fits best most churches that I know.

Paul asserts in rather blunt language that any imbalance between freedom and responsibility is perverse. Rather, he insists on the dynamic tension of love as the way to community in the midst of diverse practices with regard to food and drink: "Let not him who eats despise him who abstains, and let not him who abstains pass judgment on him who eats; for God has welcomed him. . . . Why do you pass judgment on your brother? Or you, why do you despise your brother? For we shall all stand before the judgment

seat of God. . . . Each of us shall give account of
himself to God. Then let us no more pass judgment
on one another, but rather decide never to put a
stumbling block or hindrance in the way of a brother"
(Rom. 14:3, 10, 12, 13). Paul summarized the entire
discussion: "For the kingdom of God does not mean
food and drink but righteousness and peace and joy
in the Holy Spirit; he who thus serves Christ is
acceptable to God and approved by men" (Rom.
14:17).

Isn't it time for us to take Paul seriously in this
matter? We have an arrogant way of playing God to
each other, insisting that our opinions about food and
drink came to us on tablets from heaven. We are not
called to conformity of practice but to unity of spirit.
Pushing for conformity always results in manipulation, and there can be no genuine unity as long as
we're trying to control each other. And let's face it,
uniformity is no guarantee of unity. I've been in too
many Christian circles where everyone subscribes to
the same rules but goes on sniping at each other just
the same. Christian maturity is marked by experiencing unity in diversity. It was said of the early
Christians when they were at their best, "See how they
love one another!" Too often, it can be said of us:
"See how they pick at one another!"

Let's keep these three passages of Paul in dynamic
tension! Where guilt is laid upon Christians for what
they eat and drink, strike a note for freedom
in Christ. Where freedom becomes irresponsible
and disruptive, sound the call for responsibility. And

whichever side you're on, stop playing God! And work for a climate of mutual love and respect that learns to accept diversity.

And, believe me, it's not easy to accept diversity in these matters and still maintain a climate of mutual love and respect. Paul's insistence that we do not mislead the weaker brother into sin by our example (Rom. 14:13) can be horribly abused. This takes the form of manipulation in which I press you to conform to my pattern on the grounds that your behavior might cause me to stumble. Nonsense! In Paul's argument, the weaker brother is neither the prude who is easily offended nor the pious one who insists that everyone conform to his standards. I see the weaker brother as that person standing just outside the door of faith, looking earnestly at us, on the edge of decision. To me, the weaker brother includes our children and youth upon whose impressionable minds and open hearts our attitudes and actions are being indelibly recorded.

I'm convinced that more weaker brothers get turned off by seeing our nit-picking and carping criticisms than by what some arrogant pietist chooses to label a bad example. Acting responsibly toward the weaker brother does not demand conformity of behavior as a mark of Christian community. Paul refused to take sides in the battle at Rome. Some interpret him as though he did. But he only left us with the principles of responsible freedom within diversity, knowing full well the difficulties in seeking the balance.

The net result of this is tension. Unfortunately, most of us regard tension as something to be avoided. This is a tragic misconception. Tension is essential to life. There is only one state of absolute equilibrium, and when that happens it's time for a funeral. Christian commitment does not eliminate tension in our lives, nor is the church a place where tension shouldn't exist. Tension is the mark of responsible freedom within diversity.

HOLY DAYS

After mentioning the matter of food and drink to the Colossian Christians, Paul goes on to mention festivals, new moons and sabbaths. Just as food and drink had become a source of division and bickering, so the special observance of particular seasons and days had also become a battleground. We have kept this issue alive as well as evidenced by our squabbles over what should or shouldn't be done on Sundays. It has not been uncommon in gatherings of Christian athletes for professional athletes to be confronted by: "How can you play ball on Sunday and still call yourself a Christian?"

The issue then, and now, is not that all special days and seasons be abolished. The observance of Sunday as a day for the celebration of Christ's resurrection and the Sabbath worship of God is certainly central to the historic church. There is no question here as to whether or not Christians will take seriously the importance of regular worship on the Lord's Day. That's assumed as basic. The problem occurs when Sunday or any other day is made into a legalistic fetish.

The day itself, insists Paul, is just a shadow of what is to come. Christ alone is the substance. Worship of and obedience to Christ is the reality—not the day nor the season.

FALSE HUMILITY

The third false practice Paul attacks is that of self-abasement (2:18). "Let no one disqualify you," literally means, "don't let anyone rob you of your prize." The prize, of course, is the love and presence of Jesus Christ. In him we have all of the riches and wisdom of God. What a prize! The Gnostics would take that away for the sake of following *their* wisdom instead of Christ. Self-abasement is likely a form of false humility. Here is where humility is used as a means of manipulation. It may have included fasting when done as a means of earning special favor from God. Isn't it interesting that false teaching is often built upon Christian virtues? Humility is one of the cardinal Christian virtues, exalted by Paul in Colossians 3:12. Again and again, the Christian community is exhorted to practice humility—when it is grounded in a genuine awareness that all we are and have is the gift of God to us. Paul expressed it so beautifully in Romans 12:3, "I bid every one among you not to think of himself more highly than he ought to think, but to think with sober judgment, each according to the measure of faith which God has assigned to him." False humility puts on guises in order to impress others, or worse, to make points with God. And the Gnostics insisted on that!

Haven't you witnessed this along the way? A man I knew years ago had a way of making most people around him uncomfortable. Whenever he was affirmed or congratulated his response was to credit someone else or to insist that he was just a worm for Christ. If you were entering a building together, it was impossible to be the last one through the door. But as I got to know him better, I found him to be one of the most self-righteous, manipulative persons I've ever observed—a classic case of the self-abasing, false humility of which Paul speaks.

ANGEL WORSHIP

Next, Paul refers to the worship of angels. While there is no way to be sure exactly what was going on, it probably had something to do with the concept of the emanations. Apparently, some kind of worship of angels had developed as part of the Gnostic expression. I've wondered if some of the recent flurry about demons and exorcism isn't a form of angel worship? At least, it seems to me that we err if we spend too much time and energy focusing upon the devil and the demonic. The ultimate reality is that Jesus Christ reigns supreme over all angelic beings, good and evil alike. Again, Jesus Christ alone, God in all of his fulness, can be the only focus of our worship.

Visions

Finally, Paul refers to the false teaching which gives credibility to visions. Apparently, Paul is referring to a cultic initiation in which the initiate comes to the climax of the rite by entering the sanctuary of the oracle, receiving a vision enabling him to penetrate the secrets of the universe. From that moment, he "took his stand on visions." Thus the false teachers claimed to have an esoteric experience which had given them the keys to understanding the depths of the mysteries of life.

The same thing still happens today. It's not uncommon to hear someone who claims a direct vision from God giving some special insight—often in connection with some aspect of the return of Christ. One of the basic principles to which I am committed, emphasized by Martin Luther and John Calvin, is that we are bound to Scripture alone for all of our knowledge of God. Visions that claim to take us beyond what God has revealed to us in Jesus Christ and the Bible are spurious.

So, after examining these aberrations Paul condemns them because they produce a person "puffed up without reason by his sensuous mind, and not holding fast to the Head" (2:18–19). There in just fifteen, easy-to-understand words the Apostle spotlights the two fatal results of the subtle and false teaching put out by the Colossian Gnostics. To be puffed up without reason is the opposite of true humility. Here is a picture of one bloated with pride, when in reality he is absolutely out of touch with Christ. How easy it is to be so cocksure of one's rightness, so proud of one's orthodoxy, all the while failing to realize that such pride separates us from Christ.

The second fatal result: detachment from the body of Christ. We've all heard remarkable stories of how a severed arm or leg has been restored to the body, sometimes hours after an accidental amputation. This became personal for us when one of our daughters caught her finger in a door, severing off the tip. We rushed her to the doctor, and he asked if we had brought the amputated part with us. This had not occurred to us; in fact, one of our other girls had found it and with loud "yuk" had thrown it into the bushes near the door. You should have seen us searching for that fingertip. And what a celebration when we found it. It was restored, and now except for a small scar, she has a normal finger.

Severed from the body, a member can only die. To allow issues of food and drink, holy days, false humility, angel worship, or visions to come between a person and Christ has the end result of cutting oneself off from the body. What could be more tragic?

THE INNER CIRCLE SYNDROME

In my opinion, the one thing that these practices which Paul has condemned have in common is the insatiable desire of a person to get into the inner circle. What's the first need you feel when you walk into a group where you don't know anyone? Isn't it the need to penetrate the circle of acquaintance and friendship?

We Christians have an almost diabolical proclivity for developing "inner circles." There is a danger that we unwittingly use this as a tool for evangelism. Reflecting upon my years in youth ministry, I have to admit that much of our appeal was based upon creating an "inner circle" atmosphere. If you accepted Christ you were in—you could use the key words and were warmly received. If you didn't, you were still on the outside looking in. Though we said we loved you, you were still not accepted in the inner circle. I'm convinced that this is the reason why so many kids who accept Christ in that context are the "dropouts" in later years. Luring people into Christian conversion with an over-emphasis upon social acceptance is both dangerous and unworthy.

And we can carry this inner circle syndrome well beyond conversion. How often we use the deeper life, the victorious life, or the baptism or fulness of the Holy Spirit as a carrot to bring people into our inner circle of advanced Christians. Here we offer certain spiritual experiences or secrets, guaranteed to take us a few steps beyond where most Christians are. Such approaches have a history of creating divisions rather than unity in the whole body. To be sure, they create a visible unity in the inner circle, but they exclude many others and create a sense of superiority among the "ins." A pastor friend of mine had a group of such people who, instead of worshiping with the congregation, met in another room in the church each Sunday during the service to pray that he would receive the baptism of the Holy Spirit. How arrogant—setting up an inner circle with special jargon and pious expressions, trying to lure or coerce people into our inner circle! Claiming to be loving, these approaches actually shut people out spiritually and socially—and all in the name of Christ.

Such were the tactics of the Gnostics to the Colossian Christians. And they continue today. Paul insists that Christ is all we need. If we hold fast to him, we will not need special secrets, experiences of "something more," code words, or heavenly visions. We will be able to celebrate diversity within the body of Christ without aping or coveting each other's gifts. Above all, we will not be puffed up. But we will be members of a healthy, growing body of which Christ—not our inner circle—is the head.

You Died with Christ

Paul underscores everything he has just said in the next paragraph (2:20–23). Paul patiently but emphatically reminds them again that they "died to the elemental spirits of the universe." This is the second time he uses the term *stoicheia* (see v. 8). As we observed before, in baptism their death had been proclaimed. This was one of Paul's favorite metaphors, used in Romans 6:1, 2 Corinthians 4:10, Galatians 2:20, and 2 Timothy 2:11. In Romans 7,

Paul develops the concept of our death to the Law. That death which takes place in Christ means simply that the Law has no claim upon us. Death dissolves the binding power of the relationship. Paul uses the analogy of the marriage relationship, pointing out that with the death of the partner, the lifelong bond of the marriage is dissolved. This is, of course, one of the most difficult realities that must be confronted in the process of grief. There is a natural drive that wants to keep the bond of the relationship alive.

Each week I try to contact a man who lost his wife by death after more than fifty years of marriage. He simply cannot accept the fact that she is gone. He talks with her, he does things trying to please her and refuses to dispose of any of her clothing or personal effects. I've been deeply touched by his devotion to her, but I'm also aware that he hasn't really lived since the day she died. Our grief work is not complete until we have come to the full acceptance that death really terminates the binding force of the relationship, at least as far as the day-to-day realities of life are concerned. I happen to believe that there is much more to our relationships beyond death which yet remains beyond the reach of our understanding. (If you haven't read C. S. Lewis, *The Great Divorce*, I recommend it highly.) But that doesn't change the fact that death really terminates human relationships as we know them in this life. One couple whose wedding I performed insisted on eliminating the phrase in the traditional vows: "as long as we both shall live." Again, I admire their devotion, but someday they will have to deal with the finality of death as far as this life is concerned.

Now the point that Paul is making here is powerful. In Christ we have actually died to the "elemental spirits." The force of the old rules and regulations has been killed. To go back to living by rules and regulations "according to human precepts and doctrines" is like living in bondage to someone who has died. Ours is a new life in the living Christ, not a style shaped by dead precepts.

And we really ought to remember what Jesus had to say in his criticism of the religionists of his day.

> Well did Isaiah prophesy of you hypocrites, as it is written, "This people honors me with their lips, but their heart is far from me; in vain do they worship me, teaching as doctrines the precepts of men." You leave the commandment of God, and hold fast the tradition of men. . . . There is nothing outside a man which by going into him can defile him; but the things which come out of a man are what defile him. . . . Whatever goes into a man from outside cannot defile him, since it enters, not his heart but his stomach, and so passes on. . . . What comes out of a man is what defiles a man. For from within, out of the heart of man, come evil thoughts, fornication, theft, murder, adultery, coveting, wickedness, deceit, licentiousness, envy, slander, pride, foolishness. All these evil things come from within, and they defile a man. (Mark 7:6–23).

From this we are assured that the authority of the regulations has been erased by Christ through his death on the cross. The rules are dead and have no binding power upon us. I recall vividly my confusion in the months following my conversion to Christ. The people who had been most significant in introducing

me to Christ (and I shall always love and cherish
them) did not hesitate to inform me that some of my
standards with regard to eating and drinking had to
be changed. All kinds of behavioral rules were quickly
established as part of my nurture. But as I moved
about in ever expanding circles of the Christian
family, I became increasingly bewildered by the
diversity of conflicting rules and regulations. I'll
never forget my first trip years ago into the southern
part of the United States where mixed swimming was
taboo. But smoking (high on the no-no list in my
Christian circles in Southern California) was casually
practiced by the clergy and lay persons alike. Perhaps
the sure sign of traditions that are human in origin is
their diversity.

What gives the rules and regulations their viability
is that they appear to have certain values. They DO
have an "appearance of wisdom." They seem to make
sense and obviously stand for what is right and good.
And, rules and regulations certainly promote "rigor
of devotion and self-abasement and severity to the
body" (2:23). Paul does not question the fact that
the approach to Christian discipleship which stresses
the keeping of rules seems on the surface to be
perfectly wise and legitimate. It's hard to reject
anything that appears to offer a disciplined and
controlled life, especially when it produces genuine
self-denial. Paul doesn't seem to quarrel with the basic
essence of the behavior produced by the rules. But his
concern is always focused at the point of the centrality
of Christ. Once we begin to major upon the regulations, we move Christ out of the center. Our

redemption is God-given in Jesus Christ, and no man-made rules must be allowed to take the spotlight from him.

Paul's ultimate attack on the rules approach is that "they are of no value in checking the indulgence of the flesh" (2:23). Negative, or even positive, rules simply have no power to change the underlying motivations of a person. Living by rules and regulations is like sitting on a mad dog. You may be able to control him as long as you're on top, but sooner or later, you've got to get up, and when you do, the dog just may get the upper hand. In psychological language, this is called suppression and must not be confused with repression which actually takes place at a level below our consciousness. Strong suppression, powerful self-control, based upon sheer willpower, does not deal with the underlying problem.

I recall long conversations years ago with a man prominent in professional football. As a player, he was able to bring incredible discipline and control to his performance. But basically he was an undisciplined person. He was out of control personally, emotionally, sexually, and financially. He could bring himself under control for the sixty minutes of the game, but he was unable to live well outside of the stadium. The Bible always sees the problem at its deepest level, namely, the basic rebellion of man to God's control which produces a continuing proclivity to disobedient and destructive behavior.

To be in Christ is to be dead to the demands of the rules and regulations approach to religion. Keeping the rules, no matter how productive they may be in promoting goodness and righteousness, ultimately produces a self-centered pride in one's achievements rather than a whole-souled dependence upon Jesus Christ. Until we die with Christ to the way of religion, we will never really know the joy and freedom of the new life he brings.

You Rose with Christ

In four compact sentences, Paul gives us a magnificent statement of the basic premise of the Christian life (3:1–4). He continues with the theme of death and resurrection. In Christ, we are literally dead to the appeal of the old and inadequate ways. We are now alive to a new way and a new order. Often, standing beside a person who has died, I am aware that he or she is now dead to my voice or touch. I can have no more influence or role in that person's life. But I do believe that the person is now alive to God's presence and kingdom in a new way. Paul insists that the same thing is true in our life in Christ. In Christ we have moved out of one sphere of life into another. The appeal of the old can no longer control us and we are literally raised into a new set of values based upon an entirely new perspective.

A friend of mine recently put it this way, "Frankly, the old quest for money and power, status and prestige, just doesn't turn me on anymore." The "things that are above" need not be thought of merely as other-wordly things. They are all of the things in this life that express Christ's love and compassion in human relationships. These become our new priorities and stand above all others.

Paul is here echoing the words of Jesus: " . . . do not be anxious, saying, 'What shall we eat?' or 'What shall we wear?' . . . your heavenly Father knows that you need them all. But seek first his kingdom and his righteousness, and all these things shall be yours as well" (Matt. 6:31–33). In the same passage, Jesus said, "Do not lay up for yourselves treasures on earth, where moth and rust consume and where thieves break in and steal, but lay up for yourselves treasures in heaven, where neither moth nor rust consumes and where thieves do not break in and steal. For where your treasure is, there will your heart be also" (Matt. 6:19–21).

Genuine Christian conversion produces a new set of standards and values as far reaching as the change that occurs in dying and being raised into a new life. And all of this happens in the context of becoming those who have a future contingent upon the coming appearance of Christ (v. 4).

ACTIVE DISCIPLESHIP

We must not leave this paragraph without underscoring the fact that our new life in Christ is active, not passive. Some of the worst advice given to me as a new Christian said in effect, "Just relax and let God do all the work in you." Now, the people who told me this meant well, but they were carelessly mishandling the word of God. It is true that the New Testament

makes it clear that Christ is in us and that the Holy
Spirit fills us, yet we are told in positive terms that we
are to work hard in living out active obedience to the
living God. I find no indication that Paul believed in
some kind of spiritual experience that transforms us
into victorious Christian robots under the computer-
ized control of the Holy Spirit.

Paul concludes that magnificent portion of Scripture on our freedom as Christians with two demanding and stretching imperatives: "seek" (v. 1) and "set
your minds" (v. 2). Both of these imperatives have to
do with the inner life of our thoughts and attitudes.
And believe me, that's where Christian discipleship is
won or lost!

To seek and to set our minds on spiritual things is
to establish our priorities with Christ at the pinnacle.
But how difficult that is. I've long had to accept the
conclusion that my priorities are reflected substantial-
ly in the way I use my time and money over which I
really have control. It is true that a certain amount of
our time must be spent sleeping, eating, working,
traveling, grocery shopping, answering the telephone, paying the bills, cleaning house, and even
hauling out the trash. But the time that we control
beyond the demands of necessities reflects our
ultimate values. How do we spend that time? To what
extent is it used in going after the things here and
now that I want? To what extent is it used to grow in
my relationship with Christ and to extend my love
and service to people in need?

Money, like time, is also our way of expressing our
values. Much of our money is already spent before we

get our paycheck. Housing costs, taxes, food and clothing, automobile expenses, insurance premiums, and now college tuition all combine to siphon off most of the money we manage to earn. But, in spite of the excessive demands of daily living, the responsibility for the stewardship of our money is an inescapable part of Christian discipleship. With good management, I'm convinced that each of us in American suburbia can direct significant amounts of our money to the work of Jesus Christ throughout the world if we dare to reshape our priorities around Christ and "the things that are above."

I've got to pause here and reflect on the principle of tithing as the basis of Christian stewardship. I'm amazed at the kind of nonsense and rationalization that places tithing in the same category as the dietary laws of the Old Testament—once useful but no longer valid. It is true there were many laws in the Old Testament that were uniquely needed if Israel was to survive the rigors of the Sinai wilderness. But, as I've already mentioned, thanks to modern refrigeration, most of those dietary regulations are no longer valid. There are timeless spiritual and moral absolutes given to Israel by God for us and for all time.

Jesus made this clear in the Sermon on the Mount, Matthew 5–7. The love Jesus had for the Law of God is obvious. At every point, Jesus demanded of his followers not less but more than the Law required. He led them beyond the letter of the Law to the spirit of the Law. He never said, "The former statements are inoperative." He never said, "Now that you are under grace, you can ignore the Law." His was always the way of going the second mile, the way of surpassing the minimal requirements. While Jesus never spoke to the specific question of tithing, it is inconceivable to me that he did not recognize this long established principle as valid and essential to the life of the people of God. The bringing of the first tenth of one's income to the storehouse to be used for the work of God, especially for the poor and needy, was as basic to Israel's life as eating and sleeping. It was only after the tithe, the irreducible minimum, that the offerings were given.

If we are going to "seek and set our minds on things above," can anything less than the tithe be considered as a minimum response for the Christian steward? I think not. To do this will require some drastic reshaping of values and priorities, but isn't that what Christian discipleship is all about? I believe this is the area where we will either find or lose the dynamic joy of Christian freedom.

The witness of a businessman in our church has influenced me greatly. Years ago, Peter Geddes started a printing business, and since he and his wife, Chris, had long been committed to tithing, they gave the first ten percent of their earnings to the work of Christ. A few years later, they came to the conviction that they preferred to have Christ as an equal partner in the business and committed themselves to giving fifty percent of their earnings to the Lord's work. This they have been doing for many years, and I say without reservation that in the years I've known them they stand among the happiest and most fulfilled people I know. They have chosen to live a very simple lifestyle in order to release their resources more abundantly for Christ. They'll tell you that they wouldn't have it any other way.

We can't have it both ways. Jesus insisted that we can't worship God and money. In many ways he taught us and showed us that it is in giving that we receive. The life that is going to experience the power and the glory of the risen Christ will only come when we are faithful stewards of our time and money.

SUMMARY

Paul's whole concept of the Christian life is one of dynamic tension between freedom and responsibility. This entire section of Colossians is based on this truth. On the one hand, we are free from the bondage of slavery to burdensome rules and regulations. On the other hand, we are responsible to live out that freedom in obedience to God and with care for each other. Freedom without responsibility degenerates into destructive anarchy. Responsibility without freedom becomes a stifling legalism. But the Christian life may best be described as *responsible freedom* exercised as people who have died to one way of life and who have been raised into a new way of living in Christ.

POINTS TO PONDER

1.   Do you have difficulty keeping the doctrinal
and practical in balance? On which do you tend to
major?

2.   Are there areas of your behavior in which you
are living under bondage to rules and regulations?
How do you deal with the tension between freedom
and responsibility?

3.   Have you ever wanted to be in "the inner
circle" of some religious group or experience? What
did you do about it?

4.   Describe in your own words what you feel it
means to die with Christ. To be raised with Christ.

5.   What do you feel about tithing? How important is your attitude toward money in your relationship with Christ?

6

Off with the Old,
On with the New

Colossians 3:5–17

Once again, Paul continues his line of thought with the word "therefore." The key to Christian living is found within this connective word. Paul ties the practical struggles and issues of day-to-day living directly to the death and resurrection of Christ. What a powerful picture of our new life in Christ! Yet it is so easy to miss it.

To trust in Christ is to enter into death and resurrection with him. This has nothing to do with religious experiences or emotional feelings. It is a FACT, the reality given us by God. To be in Christ is to be dead to what is past and raised alive to what is new!

It is important to read this section of Colossians in the light of its original setting. Here were people who had been raised in a pagan culture without any meaningful knowledge of God. It was a cruel world,

devoid of love or compassion; dog-eat-dog; don't
bother me with your problems; eat, drink, and be
merry if you can, tomorrow we die.

By contrast, the gospel insists there is a God who
loves us . . . by opening our lives to Jesus Christ we
can be born anew . . . repent and be baptized for
the forgiveness of your sins . . . there is a place
prepared for you . . . in my Father's house are
many rooms.

The difference between these two views of life is as
radical as the difference between old and new
clothing. Most of our family vacations have been
spent camping. We love to hike in the high country
where we can wear our old grubbies and not worry
about appearances. But we've developed one tradition. We each bring along one dress-up outfit and
choose at least one evening to go to dinner at the
nicest place we can find—sometimes driving fifty
miles or more. We always chuckle at the exhilaration
we feel as we shed our tattered clothes and dress in
comparative elegance for our night out.

I really love the precision of Paul's writing here.
Using the analogy of putting off the old clothing and
donning the new, he gives us three lists of five—two
lists of things to be put off and one list of things to be
put on.

In studying these, be sure not to fall back into the
old game of keeping rules and regulations. Paul's
central appeal here is one of urging us to be what we
really are in our death and resurrection with Christ.
He's made it clear that we have moved out of one way
of living into another. We really have died to the old.

We really have been raised into the new. Now the challenge is to be in daily practice, what we really are in God's sight. Too often, I fear, our appeals for Christian obedience sound more like exhortations to be what we are NOT rather than encouragements to be what we ARE. To Paul this was absurd! He is literally shouting out: BE WHAT YOU ARE! You are dead to the old and alive to the new. "If anyone is in Christ, he is a new creation; the old has passed away, behold the new has come" (2 Cor. 5:17). Let's look now at three lists of five.

PUT OFF THE OLD

Put to death therefore what is earthly in you: immorality, impurity, passion, evil desire, and covetousness, which is idolatry. On account of these the wrath of God is coming. In these you once walked, when you lived in them. But now put them all away: anger, wrath, malice, slander, and foul talk from your mouth. Do not lie to one another, seeing that you have put off the old nature with its practices and have put on the new nature, which is being renewed in knowledge after the image of its creator. Here there cannot be Greek and Jew, circumcised and uncircumcised, barbarian, Scythian, slave, free man, but Christ is all, and in all (Col. 3:5–11).

How often I've heard people say in recent years, "I'm sick and tired of a religion of *don'ts*. . . . Give me a positive religion!" Basically, I could not agree more, but there is another side to the coin. This might be as sensible as saying that I always want the coin to

come up heads! As surely as a coin has two sides so do
moral and ethical choices. To say yes to one option is
to say no to another.

In making decisions about behavior, negatives
become positives and positives are linked to negatives.
For example, *"Thou shalt not commit adultery,"* is
simply another way of saying *"Thou shalt be faithful to
your spouse." "Thou shalt* honor your father and your
mother"* is the same as saying *"Thou shalt not be
disrespectful. . . ."* What a waste of time to get hung
up on negatives. Reword them all into positives if you
like, but we can't escape the fact that Christian
discipleship always involves us in choices that require
clear *yeses* and *nos.* Paul's first two lists of five
characteristics of the Christian lifestyle are phrased in
the negatives "put to death" and "put away."

HANDLING OUR SEXUALITY

The first list of things to be put to death deals
primarily with our sexuality. Paul is not saying that
our sexual appetites are evil or that our bodies are to
be viewed with disdain. He is speaking directly to the
ways in which we misuse these God-given drives.
Nowhere are we closer to the culture of New
Testament times than in a discussion of sex. In all
probability Jews and Christians were the only people
in their world who believed that sexual drives were
designed by God to be used only in the context of the
total and permanent bond of monogamous marriage.

How they were chided for their narrow views! On

the top of the mountain towering above Corinth, single and married men alike stopped by the Graeco-Roman temple on their way home from work for a sexual orgy with the cultic prostitutes, presumably to the delight of the gods. In Rome, the sexual smorgasbord for heterosexuals, homosexuals, and bisexuals was everywhere present from Caesar's palace to the corner bar. In Ephesus, sexual freedom was the order of the day in the Temple of Artemis, and if you walk down the ruins today of what was once the main street, your guide will point out where the houses of prostitution flourished in the center of town. But the Christians and Jews cut across the accepted sexual mores of their time.

Aren't we in the same position? We were lulled to sleep with the idea that America was a Christian nation and came to assume that promiscuity, prostitution, and homosexuality would always be regarded as illicit and immoral, officially and unofficially. But a lot of us are feeling like Rip Van Winkle as we have awakened to the shocking discovery that our world has changed drastically while we were napping—or perhaps just looking the other way. Whether we like it or not we are back in New Testament times, at least when it comes to the sexual mores all around us.

And even church bodies are divided now on what used to be absolutes with regard to our sexuality. Our churches are torn apart over the issue of acceptance and ordination of "self-affirming, practicing homosexuals." But the ultimate issue to me is whether or not we are going to continue to affirm what the Bible has declared for more than 3,000 years—

namely, that God made us male and female, and that
the only healthy, creative, holistic, and responsible
sexual acts are those within the bonds of the marriage
covenant with chastity as the only other option. This
is clearly what the New Testament Christians and the
Old Testament Jews believed and practiced in their
day. I cannot conceive of any other option today. And
let's face it, there is no reason to believe that this view
will be any more popular today than it was then. But
after all, Jesus didn't win many popularity contests
either.

The first thing we are to put to death within us in
this sex-oriented culture is *immorality*. The word Paul
uses refers to sexual activity outside of marriage. No
matter what the latest poll may indicate the majority is
doing, the Christian is committed to the highest
standards of sexual morality. Immorality can have no
place in our lives because we have been raised with
Christ to a new quality of life.

We are also to kill the *impurity* that is within us. This
word is synonymous with immorality, emphasizing
more the lustful aspects of our sexual feelings and
attitudes. It is our desires that give birth to sexual
activity. We tend to do what we think. What we
concentrate on usually works itself out in practice.
I've never counseled with people involved in adultery
who had not first focused a lot of attention upon their
sexual longings and fantasies. And it is difficult not to
be preoccupied with sex today, not only because of
our God-given drives from within, but because of
exploitative bombardment and stimulation from
without. Probably no culture has ever lived with the

degree of eroticism that we experience matter-of-factly each day. Television, movies, newspapers, books, magazines, billboards, and clothing styles all combine to keep us sexually stimulated. Driving along the freeway, I'm invited to have a drink by a seductive, voluptuous blonde smiling from a large billboard. The appeal is based more on sex than thirst. The TV commercial urging me to buy a different brand of shaving cream is directed to my sexual drive without any hesitation whatever. Or view "Three's Company," or "Love Boat," or any of an increasing number of TV regulars; the sexual theme reigns supreme. Consequently, the gift of self-control (Gal. 5:22–23) is perhaps our most desperately needed spiritual gift. And God gives this to us as we focus upon Jesus Christ!

The third item on Paul's list is *passion.* Here the idea is that of the desire which, unchecked, leads to sexual activity apart from the commitment of marriage. Again, today as in Paul's time, so much of what we see and hear is designed to arouse the desires of passion. There's no question that for most of us, sexual desire is regularly present in some form or other. To deny it when present is likely to lead to more difficulties than dealing with it realistically. There has been a lot of unnecessary guilt in Christian circles based upon feelings. We've certainly been helped by those insights from contemporary psychology which make it clear that we really can't control the onset of many feelings. This is especially true of sexual feelings. The issue is not whether we have sexual feelings but whether we control them. Genuine control can occur only when we are able to be in touch with our feelings and honest about them.

DESIRE OUT OF CONTROL

Evil desire is used by Paul to describe passions which are out of control. The word he uses here does not refer to sexual desire alone, but to any desire for things to which we are not entitled. Sexual desire becomes evil desire if I pursue a sexual contact with anyone other than my wife. Desire for food becomes evil desire if I become overweight or if my patterns of consumption deprive others of their basic needs. Desire for clothing becomes evil desire if I allow my wardrobe to become the basis of my self-esteem or the barrier to responsible stewardship of money. Thus, any healthy, normal, and legitimate desire can become evil desire when it is not kept in proper perspective and balance in the light of our commitment to Christ.

Covetousness is a direct product of evil desire. The word we translate *covet* means "the desire to have more." Whether or not Paul intends in this sequence of five words to suggest that uncontrolled sexual drives inevitably lead to greed in general is open to question. But is there not a possible connection? I honestly believe that control in the arena of our God-given sexual drives is ultimately reflected in virtually every other area of our lives. The way in which Paul moves from the sexual to the broader area of greed shows profound insight.

Paul says in our passage that covetousness is

idolatry. What an interesting statement. We are inclined to write off idolatry as ancient, prescientific superstition, thus making it a remote possibility for us. How arrogant we are! In reality, idolatry occurs whenever we place anyone or anything higher than the will of God in our priorities. Covetousness is the greed which wants more and more. If a man covets a woman other than his wife, he will want her more and more to the point of being obsessed. At that point, he is caught in idolatry—making her into his source of ultimate fulfillment. But for most of us wealth is more likely to become our object of ultimate value. And how all consuming it can be!

Money and material possessions have a strange way of dominating our lives. When I taste something good, I want more. The more I have the more I want. The additional automobile, the second home, the next trip abroad, more in the savings account, a bigger hedge against inflation—all of these things have a way of becoming gods in our lives. But they are false gods—idols. And the problem with false gods is that they promise more than they can deliver. And I say this on good authority. John is a man of unusual gifts and abilities. I've marveled at his skills and success in business. He has become a very wealthy man, and his lifestyle makes it evident. I know many people who envy him, in fact a friend said to me, "If only I had half his wealth, I'd be the happiest person in the world." Any thought I may have had along that line was squelched when John chose to take me into his confidence. "My life is one vast wasteland," he moaned. "There's virtually nothing I want that I can't have, but the puzzle still doesn't fit together." He told me of a barren marriage held together only by spending more and more money, a palatial house that had never become a home, and a list of achievements that had become lifeless placques hanging on the wall of his den. He was running scared because he had contemplated the possibility of suicide to terminate his frustration and boredom. He obviously and desperately needs to find meaning for his life, and wealth in itself isn't the answer.

We are all more deeply infected by the virus of conspicuous consumption than we realize. But the Bible makes it quite clear that God has called us to be stewards not consumers. Something is definitely wrong when 6 percent of the world's population consumes 40 percent of the world's available resources—and then gathers in churches to thank God for being so good to us. Most of us are struggling with the problem of overweight while half of the people in the world go hungry. Senator Mark Hatfield of Oregon, Stan Mooneyham of World Vision and others have long since demonstrated to my satisfaction that the problem of world hunger is one of distribution, not shortage. Will we Christians in the Western world ever care enough to reduce our consumption and give away our wealth to feed hungry people? I doubt it. At least not until we put to death our covetousness which is idolatry.

THE WRATH OF GOD

To go on without putting to death immorality, impurity, passion, evil desire, and covetousness is to

place ourselves in the path of the wrath of God.
"Nonsense," you say, "the God of wrath is the God of
the Old Testament. Jesus has brought us the God of
love!" If this is our idea of God, it needs to be
reevaluated, because the God of Moses and the God
of Jesus are one and the same. Jesus never said, "The
former statements about the wrath of God are
inoperative." The wrath of God is the other side of his
love. God's love is never portrayed in the Bible as
mere indulgence. While God's love is unconditional,
the rejection of his love through disobedience is
always portrayed as having serious consequences.
Thus love without accountability quickly degenerates
into sloppy sentimentality, just as wrath without love
would become harshly impersonal legalism.

We who celebrate God's love and grace need to be
reminded again and again that Jesus did not come to
tell us that God is an indulgent, complacent daddy in
the sky. He is the God who requires justice and
integrity. His wrath must come upon our disobedience BECAUSE he loves us.

MASTERING OUR ATTITUDES

Paul now moves directly into his second list of five
as he continues the theme of those things we are to
put off in order to be our true selves in Jesus Christ.
Now he moves from the more external things relating
primarily to our sexuality to those pertaining to our
attitudes.

The first to be put away is *anger.* Actually the word
used here for anger refers to a continuing and

slow-burning kind of anger. The reasons for putting away this kind of anger are obvious—it burns within us to our own hurt and destruction. Slow burning, consuming anger inevitably hurts me more than the other person. In modern psychological jargon we call this resentment. In the massive tragedy of King Lear, Shakespeare has given us the classic and universal picture of the end result of unresolved anger. Lear allowed himself to be consumed with resentment to all around him. Like coals left unattended, his smoldering anger finally reduced this once giant of a man to a driveling idiot. For the sake of one's own well-being, anger must be dealt with and resolved. Holding a grudge is detrimental to one's health.

The second word in this list is translated *wrath*. This is the anger that expresses itself in an impassioned burst of temper. I'm always concerned when I hear a person define his or her temper outbursts by saying, "That's just the way I am." Not if you're risen with Christ. Expressing anger through explosive bursts is never constructive. On the other hand, learning to express anger creatively and constructively is the product of Christian maturity. And the way we express anger is learned, not inborn. Temper tantrums are learned behavior, usually carried over from childhood. But the Christ in you can liberate you from this kind of infantile behavior.

Next, Paul lists *malice*. This word has primary reference to the problems that result from evil and careless talk. I see this closely related to our contemporary put-down style. In so many ways we have become the masters of the put-down. I often feel a twinge of pain when I see the man who becomes the life of the party with his humorous but demeaning anecdotes about his wife. Humor at the expense of anyone else is sick.

Slander, likewise, has no place in the Christian lifestyle. The word Paul used to speak of this was *blasphemia,* the vilification of another by lies or careless gossip. Nothing can destroy a person or a community of believers faster than this. We tend to treat gossip lightly. Perhaps we should start calling it blasphemy to indicate how serious it really is. I witnessed the career of a clergy colleague of mine go down to destruction because of unfounded gossip about his financial affairs. While he had made the mistake in not building an adequate system of accountability into his particular type of ministry, rumors were spread about his handling of funds which simply were not grounded in fact. The far reaching effects of slander lie in ruins all around us.

Finally, *foul talk* has to go, too. Much of this we learned on the playground or in the locker room. It abounds in obscenities, most frequently referring to bodily functions. I find it refreshing occasionally to watch a late movie on TV. In my opinion, some of the greatest movies ever made were entirely free of foul talk. Somehow we've gotten into the rut of believing that powerful feelings cannot be expressed without using filthy language. But the fact is that the English language has unlimited capacity to express the whole range of human emotions without reverting to foul talk. Our current practices reflect a great deal upon our carelessness and disregard for God.

It is significant that in this list Paul relates evil speech directly to attitudes of anger and malice. This is a profound insight. Jesus certainly made this clear in Mark 7:20–23 when he said that it is the evil things that come from within us that defile us. James amplified the importance of our speech (3:1–12), pointing out that what we say is really an expression of what is within us. Thus uncontrolled anger or undisciplined sexual desires are most likely to be expressed in foul speech. In a sense, speech is a symptom of what is going on inside of us. If we are healthy within, it is most likely that our speech will be wholesome. If we are not, then foul and destructive speech will be characteristic. Thus, we best begin controlling our tongue by getting in touch with what's really going on inside of us.

I am convinced that the discipline of the tongue is one of the toughest of all to master, yet nothing is more crucial to Christian relationships. Speech that is guided by five questions cannot miss the mark very far:

1) Is it pure?
2) Is it true?
3) Is it necessary?
4) Is it kind?
5) Is it helpful?

New Persons in a New Family

In verses 9–11 of our passage Paul summarizes the reasons why all of these deadly practices must be thrown off—or put to death. They are like the old rags we wear camping. They really are out of place in a nice restaurant. These old practices just don't fit into the new life in Christ. But it's more than merely taking off the old garments—it's putting on entirely new and fresh ones, which Paul is about to describe.

But before he does, he gives us one of his classic statements of the nature of the new community now established in Christ (cf. Gal. 3:28). We not only become new *individuals* in Christ, we become part of a new *family*. All racial distinctions are abolished (Greek and Jew), and all religious differences become insignificant (circumcised and uncircumcised). Cultural differences, such as between barbarians and Scythians, are of no consequence. Scythians, by the way, were considered worse than wild beasts. And the time-honored social distinctions between slaves and free men are broken down. In Galatians, Paul insists that the traditional barriers between male and female are abolished by Christ. However, I don't hear Paul saying that these differences cease to exist in the Christian community—men remain men, women are still women, Jews are Jews, and Greeks are Greeks. Their natural differences still exist, but they are inconsequential. If we are truly one in Christ—and we are—racial, religious, cultural, social, and sexual differences are of no consequence in shaping our lives together. Why do we have such difficulty putting this into practice?

ON WITH THE NEW

Put on then, as God's chosen ones, holy and beloved, compassion, kindness, lowliness, meekness, and patience, forbearing one another and, if one has a complaint against another, forgiving each other; as the Lord has forgiven you, so you also must forgive. And above all these put on love, which binds everything together in perfect harmony. And let the peace of Christ rule in your hearts, to which indeed you were called in the one body. And be thankful. Let the word of Christ dwell in you richly, as you teach and admonish one another in all wisdom, and as you sing psalms and hymns and spiritual songs with thankfulness in your hearts to God. And whatever you do, in word or deed, do everything in the name of the Lord Jesus, giving thanks to God the Father through him (Col. 3:12–17).

The old camping clothes have been taken off and thrown away. It's time to put on our good clothing for the party—the new life in Christ. And Christ provides the new clothes for us. There are five garments that we will wear, but before we put them on it's good to pause for a moment and remember who we are: "God's chosen ones, holy and beloved" (v. 12). Paul takes all three of these titles right out of the Old Testament. And in doing so he makes it clear that now Israel doesn't mean just the ethnic descendants of Abraham, but all people of every race who are now in Christ. To be chosen by God points to a mystery beyond our understanding, but how reassuring to know. Though, as far as I can tell, I chose freely to respond to God's love, I can affirm that he chose me—and that makes it all very special.

To be called holy does not mean that I'm perfect by any means. Rather, it means that I have been set apart for the service of God; but to us, the idea of holiness is usually associated with goodness. And while goodness will certainly be the result of holiness, we must keep in mind that the root idea of holy means to be set apart. You will recall that in our discussion of the word *saints* in Colossians 1:2, vessels in the Temple were regarded as holy simply because they had been set apart for special use. So it is with people—we are holy not because we are better than others but because we have been set apart to be God's people and servants. And we are "beloved" for the same reason. God loves us, and to be loved by God becomes the source of our greatest joy.

COMPASSION

The first garment we are to wear is compassion. In attempting to understand this word in its deepest sense, I suggest that it is far more closely related to empathy than to sympathy. And there is a world of difference between the two. In sympathy we feel sorry *for* another, but in empathy we feel sorrow *with* another. Our life in Christ leads us into costly involvement with others. It's no longer enough to float above the hurts of others sprinkling down sympathy. We are called to walk *into* their hurts with them, sharing their pain and bearing their burdens. I see this kind of empathy regularly in our church family. When Bill's wife left him and insisted on a divorce, it was as though every man in that weekly prayer group had lost his wife. As Bill said to me: "In my deepest grief I never felt alone. In fact, I wasn't

alone. Those men and their wives just included me in
their families immediately. They didn't take sides or
tell me they felt sorry for me. They just kept me in
their lives." This is compassion at its best. And it's one
of the marks of genuine Christian community.

KINDNESS

The next garment is kindness. This is one of the
fruits of the Spirit in Galatians 5:22–23. To be kind is
to show genuine care for another. Kindness is
sensitivity to the feelings and hurts of the other.
Kindness gives an authentic dignity to a person
because it says, "You really matter. Your feelings and
hurts are important!" Kindness is love in action, the
cement that holds relationships together.

LOWLINESS

Along with compassion and kindness we are to
wear lowliness. Like most virtues lowliness, or humility, can be counterfeited. And the danger is that once
we have seen the phony, we will be tempted to scrap
the original. False humility hides behind a mask that
craves recognition. It is self-denial for the purpose of
manipulating others to do their bidding. Genuine
humility, by contrast, is a beautiful quality. When you
show it, you won't be aware of it. It is the kind of thing
that others will see in you—you really won't see it in
yourself. Lowliness is the companion of a healthy

self-love, and only a wholesome love of self can produce a genuine concern for the well-being of others, and that is true humility.

Meekness

Next, Paul lists meekness. Again the image of the counterfeit is valid. From boyhood, my image of meekness was shaped by a comic strip character, Casper Milquetoast. He was characteristically more of a mouse than a man, and in today's vernacular was in desperate need of assertiveness training. However, in the New Testament, meekness is not the opposite of assertiveness. Quite the contrary! Meekness is quite assertive. But it is just as insistent about the rights of others as it is about its own. I think of meekness as quiet strength. When a person is meek, there is a willingness to waive personal rights when such action is truly helpful for another. And that demands much more strength and courage than asserting one's own rights at every point.

Patience

And the last garment Paul says we are to put on is patience. Patience is the endurance of wrong without flying into a rage or demanding vengeance. Patience may be closely related to tolerance, but it is not the same. Patience works things through. It does not necessarily accept things as they are, but it works for change with deep sensitivity to the needs and interests of people.

Paul gives us an amplified definition of patience in verse 13. Patience is forbearing and forgiving. And these we do with the awareness that this is how God relates to us. We are to handle conflicts and failures in our relationships with others as God handles them in our relationship with him. He is forbearing. I take that to mean that he bears with us in our strengths and weaknesses, in our good days and bad days. He is forgiving. As long as I am honest with myself, I am always aware that my relationship with God is totally grounded in my need for his forgiveness. Because he is forbearing and forgiving with me, I am called to be the same with you—and you with me.

DYNAMICS OF FORGIVENESS

The constant need for patience and forgiveness in daily relationships mustn't be minimized. Human relationships that endure are built upon mutual need for forgiveness. By contrast, we try to ground our relationships in compatibility, mutual satisfaction, physical or intellectual attraction, common interests, or any number of such things. But I believe that the ultimate basis for a lasting relationship is found in the truth that we will need to forgive and be forgiven in order to love and to grow. Base a friendship or marriage on this and you have something very special going!

But before this can really happen in day-to-day

living, we've got to do some straight thinking about
the dynamics of forgiveness. I am afraid that we
sometimes blur the distinction between God's love
and his forgiveness. Hopefully, we know that God's
love is unconditional. He loves us—that is, he cares
for us and acts in our best interest—no matter what.
He loves us whether or not we love him. He loves us
when we obey. He loves us when we rebel. But if we
regard forgiveness as unconditional we miss the
point. When God spoke to Israel through the prophet
Jeremiah, he called them to return to him: "Return,
faithless Israel, says the Lord. I will not look on you in
anger, for I am merciful, says the Lord; I will not be
angry for ever" (Jer. 3:12). But the invitation didn't
end there. "Only acknowledge your guilt, that you
rebelled . . . and that you have not obeyed my
voice" (Jer. 3:13). The message of the prophets, the
message of Jesus, and the message of Paul are all the
same at this point. Repentance is the condition of
God's forgiveness. While Christ's death makes forgiveness available to all, there can be no forgiveness
without repentance.

And from a very practical, down-to-earth point of
view, we need to be clear about the meaning of
repentance. Repentance is not a feeling. It is an
action. Feeling sorry for our sins may lead us to
repentance, but in itself it is not repentance. Repentance is turning from our rebellion to become obedient to God. It is turning toward God whether we
feel like it or not. It is a radical change of direction.
Forgiveness cannot be a reality apart from this basic
change in direction. Incidently, here is the key to

forgiveness in human relationships as well. If you have ever tried to work out forgiveness with another person without repentance, you know the frustration that results. I have seen it again and again in couples with whom I have counseled.

Harry was always the life of the party. But he invariably drank too much and said and did things that embarrassed and hurt his wife. Every morning after a party, he dutifully asked her forgiveness. She came to me with the question, "Do I really have to put up with this forever just because he asks to be forgiven?" We really have to convince him that unless there is a change in the behavior pattern there really can't be forgiveness. This is not to say that Harry has to be perfect from here on out. But there must be some evidence of working for change.

One additional thing needs to be said about forgiveness—it is not forgetting! How often I hear a person say, "I can forgive, but I can't forget." Precisely! Forgiving is something I can do. Forgetting is something over which I have little control. If you are not convinced, stand in the corner for the next five minutes and forget that I told you not to think of pink elephants.

Like repentance, forgiveness is not a feeling you have for another, it is how you act. Forgiveness chooses to sustain and nurture the relationship even with the memory of the hurt. Forgiveness never says, "It doesn't matter." If Harry's wife had said it didn't matter and really meant it, one of two things would have been true. Either his behavior at the party wasn't

really hurting her, or he was not important enough in her life to cause her real pain. If it didn't matter, forgiveness wouldn't be needed. Forgiveness knows that it does matter and that it really cannot be forgotten. And when there is genuine turning, forgiveness goes on loving and caring, knowing that it will be needed again and again.

Wouldn't it be ridiculous to think that we could come to a place where we would never again need God's forgiveness? Why can't we bring the same reality to all of our relationships with each other?

LOVE—THE OUTER GARMENT

There is yet one more garment needed to hold all of the others together. It is *love*. This is the outer garment to be put on over and around all the rest. Love is the uniting dynamic that brings harmony to all of the other qualities of the Christian life. And this love is the self-giving love that we learn in Christ and receive from him. What is the quality of life in our new clothes really like? Life so clothed with compassion, kindness, lowliness, meekness, and patience, enclosed by the binding force of love will be characterized by *peace* and *gratitude*. The very peace of Christ will rule within us. This peace is not the absence of conflict. It is inner poise in the midst of the storms of life. And so to live is the source of continuing gratitude. To know Christ is to be thankful.

The Word of God

In verses 16 and 17, Paul gives us one more summary statement of our life together in Christ— the word of Christ is to dwell in us richly; the word of God is the source of our nurture and guidance. Psalm 119 offers the classic celebration of the power and importance of the word of God. "How can a young man keep his way pure? By guarding it according to thy word" (v. 9). "I have laid up thy word in my heart, that I might not sin against thee" (v. 11). "Thy testimonies are my delight, they are my counselors" (v. 24). "It is good for me that I was afflicted, that I might learn thy statutes" (v. 71). "The law of thy mouth is better to me than thousands of gold and silver pieces" (v. 72). "If thy law had not been my delight, I should have perished in my affliction" (v. 92). "Thy word is a lamp to my feet and a light to my path" (v. 105). "I hate double-minded men, but I love thy law" (v. 113). "The unfolding of thy words gives light; it imparts understanding to the simple" (v. 130).

Life Together

With regularity, the Christian community must gather for teaching, admonishing, and singing. In teaching, we are to draw out the meaning of the Scriptures for our lives. Preaching and teaching that does not seek to interpret the Scriptures simply has no place in the Christian community.

In Christian community, we are to enter into responsible relationships with one another. The concept of the typical church congregation composed of people coming and going as they please is quite foreign to the New Testament. The church of God's design is an intentional community of people who hold themselves accountable to God *and to each other.* How to bring that about in a large congregation remains a bit of an enigma to me, but I believe it can happen in small groups that meet regularly for prayer, sharing, and Bible study, becoming responsible to one another.

And Christians just have to sing when they are together! I take the reference to psalms, hymns, and spiritual songs to indicate the rich diversity of our musical heritage. I know some folks who are very suspicious of any church music written after the nineteenth century. But I also have some young friends who are not aware that there was any Christian music before 1965! Until we have learned to celebrate with the great music of all periods, we have really impoverished ourselves.

Such teaching, admonition, and singing will penetrate every dimension of our lives. Jesus simply cannot be confined to a religious corner of our lives. To speak and live in the name of Jesus is to allow his presence and power to infuse everything we are and do and say. To live in any other way is to deprive ourselves of the vast resources of God.

SUMMARY

In these remarkable paragraphs, Paul has portrayed the beauty and power of the Christian lifestyle. He has called us to take off the old, tattered clothes of our previous ways and to dress in clothes fit for the party to which Christ calls us. The new clothing is satisfying and liberating, making deep and meaningful relationships possible at every level of life.

POINTS TO PONDER

1.   What is your understanding of the meaning of each of these terms: immorality, impurity, passion, evil desire, covetousness? How have you experienced them?

2.   Identify some specific ways in which you have experienced anger, wrath, malice, slander, or foul talk this past week.

3.   How do you or can you "put off" some of these things?

4.   Which of the five positive virtues is most attractive to you? Which do you find most difficult to achieve?

5.   How do you feel about the statement: "You just have to forgive and forget?"

6.   What parts of corporate worship do you find most meaningful? Least meaningful?

7

Life as It's Meant to Be

Colossians 3:18–4:18

The Christian faith, from beginning to completion is about relationships. From the opening chapters of Genesis to the last chapter of Revelation, the Bible deals with relationships. It opens with the profound insight that God's creative work places man at the heart of the universe for relationship with Him and with each other. In some mysterious way even God is relational within himself in the language of Genesis: "Let *us* make man in *our* own image, after *our* likeness" (Gen. 1:26, italics mine).

The first command God gave to the man and the woman was to "be fruitful and multiply" (Gen 1:28), which just can't happen without a relationship. But before the curtain falls on the first act, the drama becomes one of broken relationships. The man and the woman are hiding from God in fear because of their disobedience. When God finds them, they are estranged from each other and from nature. Adam blames Eve, Eve blames the serpent (certainly with a

sneer toward Adam), and together they lose paradise
and begin to experience nature as a foe. And to cap it
all, Adam blamed God: "This woman *you* gave me."

The stage setting for all of history is paradise
lost—humankind created for meaningful relationships with God, with each other, and with nature, but
experiencing through stubborn disobedience, aliena-
tion, conflict, and destruction. The drama continues
to this day, and at the center of the saga is Jesus
Christ. In him the broken relationships are healed,
and in God's appointed time the curtain shall fall and
rise for the last time and paradise shall be restored.
The Bible closes with all relationships restored and
alive:

> Then I saw a new heaven and a new earth; for the first
> heaven and the first earth had passed away, and the sea
> was no more. And I saw the holy city, new Jerusalem,
> coming down out of heaven from God, prepared as a
> bride adorned for her husband; and I heard a great
> voice from the throne saying, "Behold, the dwelling of
> God is with men. He will dwell with them, and they shall
> be his people, and God himself will be with them; he will
> wipe away every tear from their eyes, and death shall be
> no more, neither shall there be mourning nor crying nor
> pain any more, for the former things have passed away"
> (Rev. 21:1–4).

In this closing section of Colossians, Paul applies all
that has been said in this magnificent letter to the
basic relationships which make up our lives. From
3:18 to 4:1 he holds before us a new quality for our
marriages, our families, and our vocations. In 4:2–6

he portrays the relation of the Christian community
to the world of unbelief around it. And the letter
closes (4:7–18) with a beautiful portrait of some of the
warm, loving relationships at the core of that little
band of first-century Christians.

A NEW QUALITY OF MARRIAGE

Wives, be subject to your husbands, as is fitting in the
Lord. Husbands, love your wives, and do not be harsh
with them (Col. 3:18–19).

It would appear that the world of the Colossians
was one in which women had no place other than
bearing children and performing domestic service.
Barring either of these, prostitution or slavery may
have been the only options. One of the common
Rabbinic prayers began each day thanking God that
"I am not a dog, a Gentile, or a woman." The birth of
a daughter was hardly a cause of celebration, and a
couple without a son was an object of pity. To this
day, in Muslim lands, a woman who has not produced
a son can be divorced. That's hard to believe by us
moderns who know that the male sperm determines
the sex of the offspring. I was never more aware of
the ancient view of women than on a recent trip to
Afghanistan. I was invited to dinner in the home of a
wealthy merchant in Kabul. I was immediately aware
that there were no women present but thought little
of it until we were served by two of the teen-age sons.
As they came and went from the kitchen I wondered

who was preparing the food. Not until the meal was over did I really know. As we left the home, my host's wife and daughters were invited to the door. We were introduced and said farewell at the same time. Frankly, I found it depressing to witness a culture in which women are still relegated to subservient roles.

From some interpretations of Paul I have heard lately, I get the disturbing feeling that there are those who think that the Bible requires us to return to this ancient view of the place of women. But I believe that such a reading of Paul misses the whole point. We cannot read this passage in Colossians without putting it alongside Paul's more expanded statement in Ephesians:

Be subject to one another out of reverence for Christ. Wives, be subject to your husbands, as to the Lord. For the husband is the head of the wife as Christ is head of the church, his body, and is himself its Savior. As the church is subject to Christ, so let wives also be subject in everything to their husbands. Husbands, love your wives, as Christ loved the church and gave himself up for her, that he might sanctify her, having cleansed her by the washing of water with the word, that he might present the church to himself in splendor, without spot or wrinkle or any such thing, that she might be holy and without blemish. Even so husbands should love their wives as their own bodies. He who loves his wife loves himself. For no man ever hates his own flesh, but nourishes and cherishes it, as Christ does the church, because we are members of his body. "For this reason a man shall leave his father and mother and be joined to his wife, and the two shall become one." This is a great mystery, and I take it to mean Christ and the church (Eph. 5:21–32).

We know without a doubt that the Christian faith brought something dramatically new to the view of marriage commonly held in those days. We have become so accustomed to the influence of the Christian view across the centuries that we are likely to miss its controversial impact in places like Ephesus and Colossae in the first century. Merely to have told wives to be subject to their husbands would not have created a ripple. But to begin by calling a couple in marriage to "BE SUBJECT TO ONE ANOTHER" would have been as shocking as a ham at a bar mitzvah!

The new subjection that the gospel introduces is the subjection of love by a husband to his wife. This radical departure from traditional male dominance came directly and uniquely from Jesus himself. That's why Paul uses the analogy of Christ and the church as the new model for marriage. Christ subjected himself to the church in love. The love of Christ is a sacrificial love that gives itself to the loved one. Never before had husbands been called to bring sacrificial love to their wives. The ground of mutual subjection in marriage is that kind of self-giving love by the husband, and subjection in response to that kind of love by the woman is not a bondage but a joy.

We violate the spirit of this passage if we make this into a debate about authority in marriage. The question is not, "Who's in charge?" The question is, "Who initiates love?" And Paul makes it quite clear—as Christ initiated self-giving love for the church, so the husband is to be the initiator of that same kind of love for his wife. As the church responds in subjecting love to Christ, so the wife is to respond to her husband.

This was a radically refreshing basis for a new quality of life in Paul's day. I think it's just as new and refreshing in ours! There's no reason for carrying the dominant-male, passive-female concept into our marriages unless a particular couple wants it that way. To be sure, authority questions must be resolved in every marriage, but I find no set pattern required by the Bible. The ultimate authority in every relationship is Jesus Christ. I've often said that there's only one Lord of our manor, and I'm glad it's Christ.

COUNSEL FOR CHILDREN AND PARENTS

Children, obey your parents in everything, for this pleases the Lord. Fathers, do not provoke your children, lest they become discouraged (Col. 3:20–21).

Paul uses the same approach to family life that he did to marriage. To tell children to obey their parents hardly needed to be written. I doubt that there has ever been a time or place in which parents have not required obedience of children—at least until recent times in our culture. Grace and Fred Hechinger wrote a book a few years ago titled *Teen-Age Tyranny.* In it they pointed out the ways in which American parents are taking their cues from teen-agers. When boys went to longer hair styles, it wasn't long before dad followed. And don't gloat too soon, mom, because your skirt lengths have been going up and down with those of the teen-age girls. And who really started the trend to Levis and weird shoes?

I'm not saying that fashion is the issue, but it may be symbolic not only of our excessive permissiveness but of the greater tragedy of a generation of insecure parents desperately seeking the approval of adolescents. And the kids are the losers. Some recently published research by Diana Baumrind of the University of California, Berkeley, more than substantiates what the Bible said long ago. For almost twenty years, she has been conducting a major investigation into how various types of parental discipline affect children's behavior. Studying three small groups of normal preschool children and their parents, her findings were summarized in a pamphlet prepared by The National Institute of Mental Health:

—The most assertive, self-reliant, and self-controlled children had parents who were controlling, demanding, communicative, and loving. Rather than ridiculing or frightening the child, or withdrawing their affection, these parents were ready to use corporal punishment. Generally, though, instead of punishing a child for behaving badly, they rewarded him for behaving well.

—The children who were discontented, withdrawn, and distrustful had parents who were relatively controlling but also detached.

—The children who had little self-control or self-reliance

and who tended to retreat from new experiences had parents who were relatively warm but also non-controlling and nondemanding.

These and other studies make a strong case for the fact that firm parental discipline makes for competent children.

Our children need to learn obedience to God. The family, by God's design, is where this can best be learned. And don't forget that Paul is addressing a family in which both parents are obedient to Christ and mutually subject to one another. As we model our obedience to God as husband and wife, we are in the position to show our children the meaning of obedience which is not a burden to bear but a source of liberation and joy. As John put it so beautifully, "For this is the love of God, that we keep his commandments. And his commandments are not burdensome" (1 John 5:3).

The same studies on the effect of parental discipline on children conclude that there are three main types of parents: authoritarian, permissive, and authoritative. The *authoritarian* parent sees discipline and obedience as an end in itself and can be characterized as saying, "You'll do it because I say so!" The *permissive* parent swings to the other extreme and in the name of affirmation removes virtually all restraints. Both the authoritarian and permissive styles consistently produce confused and troubled children. *Authoritative* parents strive continually for firm, consistent, issue-oriented discipline, listening to the child but not always basing decisions on the child's desires. The authoritative style is clear about standards and open to reason. It is most likely to produce children who are competent and loving.

Now comes the other side of the coin. While telling the children to obey parents was old hat, requiring something of parents was new and bold. This is the new dimension that the gospel brings. Fathers are told to treat their children with love and care. The words of Paul to the Ephesians amplify his sentence here: "Fathers, do not provoke your children to anger, but bring them up in the discipline and instruction of the Lord" (Eph. 6:4).

I remember being told once by my grandfather, "Children are made to be seen, not heard." But I hear Paul saying, "Children are to be seen and heard and cared for." This is the unique contribution of the gospel to family life. As parents, we do well to begin with the recognition that our children really belong to God and not to us. God places them under our care for a few years and entrusts us with their nurture and training. In their obedience to us they best learn the discipline of the Lord. As they grow, they become our young brothers and sisters in Christ. I know that in our case we are finding deep joy with our two teen-age daughters as they have now become our sisters in Christ, fellow pilgrims in our Christian journey.

The family is the primary place in God's design where children are to find encouragement, love, security, affirmation, training, and discipline. This is our responsibility and privilege as parents. Such a quality of life cannot happen without time together.

Absentee fathers and mothers simply can't pull it off.
I see the church as the larger family where the work
of the family is complemented and supplemented.
But these will never be an adequate substitute for
fathers and mothers who spend quality time with
their children.

CHRIST IN THE MARKETPLACE

Slaves, obey in everything those who are your earthly
masters, not with eyeservice, as men-pleasers, but in
singleness of heart, fearing the Lord. Whatever your
task, work heartily, as serving the Lord and not men,
knowing that from the Lord you will receive the
inheritance as your reward; you are serving the Lord
Christ. For the wrongdoer will be paid back for the
wrong he has done, and there is no partiality. Masters,
treat your slaves justly and fairly, knowing that you also
have a Master in heaven (Col. 3:22–4:1).

It's always harder to experience Christ in our work
than in our marriages and families. But Paul applies
the Christian life as much to one as the other. That
shouldn't surprise us, for the central theme of Paul
was "Christ in you!" Therefore, Christ is just as much
concerned about the quality of our vocational life as
he is with our families.

Interestingly, almost half of what Paul says in this
section is addressed to slaves, more by far than to
husbands, wives, parents, children, or masters. While
we shouldn't make too much of this, I like to think
that this proportion reveals Paul's special love for
slaves who had become Christians. To become a new

person in Christ would make it all the more difficult to remain a slave, wouldn't it? We have seen how Paul regarded the person in Christ as liberated to a new freedom. But how do you talk freedom language if you're a slave?

Here we have to ponder a question that troubles those who would make Jesus or Paul fit their image of social activists. If Paul was serious about human rights and freedom, why didn't he strike a blow right here for the abolition of slavery? Was he afraid of the slave owners? I don't pretend to know what went on inside of Paul, but I believe he showed more wisdom and better judgment than appears on the surface. Paul cared for the well-being of people as well as their rights. This is quite clear from what he says to slaves and masters.

Though the institution of slavery has never yet been fully eliminated from the face of the earth, I think you can make a strong case for the fact that the Christian gospel when fully applied has done more to break the back of slavery than any other movement or ideology. And the principles that Paul establishes here will ultimately restore full human rights, even in a culture whose economic system was based upon slavery.

I've already pointed out the likelihood that Philemon was a brother in the Christian community at Colossae. If so, Paul's words to slaves and masters would have special meaning to the Colossians, for now both Philemon the master and Onesimus the slave are fellow disciples in a community in which there is neither slave nor free (3:11).

Briefly, let's recall the story as told in Philemon.

Onesimus, whose name meant "useful," had run away and become one of the vast number of fugitive slaves roaming the Mediterranean world. Far from finding freedom, the runaway slave ended up in another kind of bondage as one of the dregs of a heartless society. Then somehow, Onesimus had come in contact with Paul and had become a new man in Christ. It was agreed that it would be in the best interests of Onesimus to return to the household of Philemon, still a slave, but now as a brother in Christ. Paul writes the letter to Philemon, demanding that Onesimus be received, not as a fugitive to be punished, but as a brother to be loved. While the institution of slavery was not brought down, the quality of relationships was transformed, and I would support Paul in his choice of the best option available in that situation.

EMPLOYERS AND EMPLOYEES

A further look at our Scripture passage reveals that while we are no longer trapped in the vise of slaves and masters, thanks to the dynamics of the gospel, the words of Paul apply equally to the world of employer and employees. If these simple principles were applied in our world of collective bargaining, there would be far fewer impasses between labor and management.

Paul boldy demands a new quality of work from slaves and a new quality of leadership from masters. Now apply this to labor and management, assuming we are dealing with Christian workers and managers.

Work is to be done "as serving the Lord and not men." The gospel infuses work with dignity. The person in Christ does not work just to make a living. Work becomes the way we serve the Lord through our vocation.

A great deal of research has been done in recent years in the field of motivation. The work of Frederick Herzberg in 1959 surprised many by demonstrating that money was not one of the highest factors in motivation. Satisfaction with one's job in the sense of finding meaning in one's work has long been recognized as one of the most significant sources of motivation. What higher satisfaction could come in any work than the feeling of serving the Lord? If there isn't something in your work that you feel is in some way serving the Lord, you might need to consider a change. I tried this out once on my father who was a bus driver. He came to love his work, though it never paid very much, because he felt he was serving the Lord by helping people get to work, visit friends, and move about. Any job worth doing ought to have that feeling about it.

The Christian manager has a deep responsibility for those who work for him. Employees are to be treated "justly and fairly." Even top-level management must never forget that there is a "Master in heaven" to whom they are accountable. I've often heard executives declare their responsibility to the stockholders, and if I were a stockholder I'd certainly cheer that. I hope they'll be as aware of their responsibilities to the Lord to treat their employees justly and fairly.

Because I live and work mostly with managers and
executives, I'm especially sensitive to the box they're
in. I'm in the same bind as a member of a local school
board. Collective bargaining begins by creating an
adversary position between management and labor.
Bargaining is based upon the adversary concept. As
long as that's the case, I see no way to apply fully these
Christian principles. Both labor and management
have to share the blame for this system. All I hope for
is that where Christians are involved we will do our
best to operate in a climate of integrity and openness
that might slowly but surely change the system.

There are no quick or easy answers to the complex
questions of relationships between employees and
employers. But I'm convinced that workers who work
as serving the Lord and managers who manage justly
and fairly under Divine authority will be catalysts for
change.

Relationships with the World around Us

Continue steadfastly in prayer, being watchful in it with
thanksgiving; and pray for us also, that God may open to
us a door for the word, to declare the mystery of Christ,
on account of which I am in prison, that I may make it
clear, as I ought to speak. Conduct yourselves wisely
toward outsiders, making the most of the time. Let your
speech always be gracious, seasoned with salt, so that you
may know how you ought to answer every one (Col.
4:2–6).

Without falling into the trap of doing things merely

for the sake of appearances, the Christian community must be concerned with how we are seen by the world around us. This doesn't mean that we should be wrapped up in self-concern about displaying our piety. Paul would have nothing of the sort. We've done an exercise in some of our leadership groups in the church in which we develop a list of what we feel people perceive our church to be. People in La Canada drive by our church, see it across the street from the main shopping plaza, read about us in the local newspapers, and hear the members of our congregation talk about us. We've concluded that there's a significant gap between what they perceive and what we would like them to know about us.

To narrow the gap, we know that we have to be very clear as to the quality of our programs, communications, lifestyle, and everything else where we intersect their lives. We find Paul's guidance right to the point.

Our central purpose must never be emasculated. We are to pray and to watch for that open "door for the word, to declare the mystery of Christ." There's no point in declaring the word when the door isn't open, but most of us aren't so aggressive as to make that error. The greatest tragedy occurs when a door is opened but no sure word of Christ is proclaimed. But in our Scripture we find Paul in prison, praying for an open door, not in order to escape, but through which he could proclaim the word of Christ. How's that for a clear sense of purpose?

We must pray for the sensitivity to see those open doors. Someone new moves on the block—an open door for friendship. Sickness or death comes to a neighbor—an open door for compassion and love. A neighbor's son is picked up on a drug charge, a friend's daughter is pregnant—an open door for support and assurance. A friend is faced with unemployment—an open door for help and affirmation. A person with alcohol problems is crying out—an open door for healing. A casual conversation indicates frustration and a lack of meaning in life—an open door for sharing one's faith. Doors are opening—and closing—all around us.

You might look at all the open doors around you and say, "I just don't have time today—maybe next week." But those doors often close as fast as they opened. The word Paul uses in verse 5 is a word meaning "the opportune time, the right moment." I have long since learned that in most human needs and crises there is a particular moment like no other moment when help is needed. The management of our time is of the essence if we are going to move wisely into the open doors. Wise conduct toward those around us is inseparable from the use of our time and the quality of our conversations. Time is the most democratic of all our assets—I have just as much each day as the President of the United States. He has no more to spend than I do.

GRACIOUS SPEECH

The quality of our conversations in all of these relationships is also crucial. Our speech is to be gracious. Gracious speech is the product of active and sensitive listening. Christian witness can be ungracious if we are answering questions not being asked or giving advice not being sought. One psychiatrist used the phrase, "listening with the inner ear." If we can learn to do that, we'll hear things that weren't even said and understand better what is said. Only when we listen well can we hope to speak graciously, respecting and accepting the other's feelings.

SALTY SPEECH

Our speech is to be salty as well as gracious. I once had a hard time linking these together. During World War II in my pre-Christian days, I was a drill instructor in the Marine Corps, and I had a reputation for salty speech. But I have discovered that salty speech means something quite different here. For Paul, salt had three basic functions. It was used most extensively as a preservative. With no refrigeration, salt was virtually the only way to preserve fish or other perishable foods. Salt was also used as a purifier for sanitary purposes. And I assume that it was also used for flavoring.

All three of these uses of salt have rich meaning with regard to salting our speech. I find a hunger everywhere for conversation that preserves the joy, dignity, and wonder of life. There is so much talk around us that tears down, belittles, and destroys, but our speech should build up and preserve. Conversation that cleanses and purifies is also greatly needed.

Talk that stains and smears is unworthy of the
Christian disciple. And hopefully our conversation
will have the zest and flavor that brings out the best in
people. Too often we have colored "Christian" dull
gray. How sad!

Through prayer, gratitude, sensitivity, and gra-
ciousness we are to major upon high quality relationships with those not yet in the family of Christ. We
must avoid becoming defensive, huddling in safe
Christian ghettos. Rather, we are to be on constant
watch for open doors through which the gospel can
be shared in our behavior and in our conversations,
that the whole world may know that Jesus Christ is
Lord.

THE INNER CIRCLE OF PAUL'S FRIENDS

Tychicus will tell you all about my affairs; he is a
beloved brother and faithful minister and fellow servant
in the Lord. I have sent him to you for this purpose, that
you may know how we are and that he may encourage
your hearts, and with him Onesimus, the faithful and
beloved brother, who is one of yourselves. They will tell
you of everything that has taken place here.

Aristarchus my fellow prisoner greets you, and Mark
the cousin of Barnabas (concerning whom you have
received instructions—if he comes to you, receive him),
and Jesus who is called Justus. These are the only men of
the circumcision among my fellow workers for the
kingdom of God, and they have been a comfort to me.
Epaphras, who is one of yourselves, a servant of Christ
Jesus, greets you, always remembering you earnestly in

his prayers, that you may stand mature and fully assured in all the will of God. For I bear him witness that he has worked hard for you and for those in Laodicea, and in Hierapolis. Luke the beloved physician and Demas greet you. Give my greetings to the brethren at Laodicea, and to Nympha and the church in her house. And when this letter has been read among you, have it read also in the church of the Laodiceans; and see that you read also the letter from Laodicea. And say to Archippus, "See that you fulfil the ministry which you have received in the Lord."

I, Paul, write this greeting with my own hand. Remember my fetters. Grace be with you (Col. 4:7–18).

For a long time I used to skim the concluding greetings of Romans and Colossians with all the enthusiasm I might feel reading the telephone book while waiting for a connecting flight in Omaha. Then I discovered what I was missing! In these greetings we learn a lot about the quality of relationships within this motley band of believers. Brought together by the living Christ, they did a lot of living together. And the warmth and depth of their relationships bring us the hope that we can experience the same quality in ours.

Paul concludes this beautiful letter referring to ten of his friends. And through these friends we learn much about Paul, for a man is known in part by the friends he treasures. *Tychicus* and *Onesimus* were chosen to be the messengers bearing the letter to Colossae. They were obviously special friends to merit such trust. Tychicus had been a companion of Paul after he returned to Asia from Greece (Acts

20:4) and often served as a special messenger for Paul
(2 Tim. 4:12; Titus 3:12; Eph. 6:21). What greater
tribute could he have had than being called "beloved
brother, faithful minister, and fellow servant in the
Lord" by Paul. He models the friend who is always
there, ready to deliver a message, eager to serve with
very little recognition. All of us need people like
Tychicus around, people who take seriously that most
overlooked gift of the Spirit, the gift of helping!

We have already met Onesimus, Philemon's runaway slave. Perhaps Onesimus was also carrying
Paul's letter to Philemon, or this may have been a
later journey. At any rate, Onesimus had become a
special friend and brother to Paul, one of his "sons" in
Christ. One of the great rewards in helping another
person come to know Christ is the lifelong relationship of love and gratitude that often follows.

Aristarchus is the next to be mentioned. He bore the
scars of battle along with Paul. We first meet him
being dragged through the streets of Ephesus in the
riot that resulted when Paul's preaching became a
threat to the silversmiths in the Temple of Artemis
(Acts 19:29). He was a companion of Paul on the final
journey to Rome. In prison with Paul as this letter was
written, Aristarchus was the kind of friend who never
turned back.

The mention of *Mark* would have been shocking to
many. This was clearly John Mark with whom Paul
had a real blow up. John Mark had been assigned to
assist Paul and Barnabas on their first missionary
journey from Antioch (Acts 13:5). He left them in
Pamphylia to return to Jerusalem (Acts 13:13) in

what Paul regarded as desertion (Acts 15:38). After Paul and Barnabas had completed their first journey, they returned to Antioch. As they were about to embark upon their second missionary venture, Barnabas wanted to take his nephew Mark with them again (Acts 15:36–40). Paul was so adamant in his refusal to have anything to do with a deserter that he broke with Barnabas and shipped out with Silas. Barnabas then took Mark with him, so in God's good providence the split resulted in two missionary teams instead of just one. But the hostility between Paul and Mark was sharp. Here and in 2 Timothy 4:11 it is clear that there had been reconciliation and healing of this broken relationship.

I find this both comforting and challenging. It is comforting because it tells us that even the early apostles had their conflicts and fallings-out. I am glad that the writers of Scripture never covered up those weaknesses and failures. And it is challenging in the reminder that we should always seek the healing of broken relationships. How Paul and Mark, and presumably Barnabas, ever get together again we'll never know. But they did! Perhaps we all have some relationships out of our past that deserve a try at reconciliation. To do that somebody has to say, "I'm sorry!"

Jesus Justus is one of those unheralded and unknown heros of that little band. Jesus was a very common name, so he was identified as Justus. But even then we know nothing of him other than that he was one of the three Jewish Christians in Paul's inner circle who was a source of comfort to Paul. So much of our Christian heritage has been shaped by those unknown quiet giants.

Epaphras was a Colossian who had gone to be with Paul and whose concerns gave rise to this letter. The Colossians were most fortunate to have an Epaphras who cared so deeply and who continued to hold them in his prayers. Every church is dependent on people who care and pray like him.

Luke and *Demas* were with Paul and sent their greetings with the letter. What a contrast! It is hard to believe that their names were mentioned in the same breath. Luke, the beloved physician, Paul's companion and friend and brilliant writer of the Gospel and Acts. Where would we be without him? And Demas? All we know is that he became a dropout. "For Demas, in love with this present world, has deserted me" (2 Tim. 4:10). How sad! One day he stands alongside Luke and Paul. Later, he chooses comfort and security instead. Demas stands as a constant reminder of the truth of the adage, "Let anyone who thinks that he stands, take heed lest he fall" (1 Cor. 10:12). We must trust Christ one day at a time, always aware of our complete dependence upon him.

Nympha was one of the many women who was the backbone of the early church. Long before the building of structures, the churches gathered in homes like Nympha's for their fellowship, nurture, and worship. In similar fashion many of us today are discovering the power of meeting in small groups in our homes. I know for a fact that the vitality of the large congregation in our church on Sunday morning is a direct product of all of those little gatherings during the week.

At the conclusion of this paragraph, Paul suggests that they exchange letters with the Laodiceans, indicating that he was writing to them at the same time. The letter to be exchanged from Laodicea has never been found. In fact, the only thing we know about the church in Laodicea is the sad commentary on its lukewarmness (Rev. 3:14–22). Like the Demases who drop out, once great churches can also fall away.

Paul closes the letter with a word of exhortation to *Archippus* to fulfill his ministry. We meet Archippus in Philemon 2, and some have suggested that he was Philemon's son. Perhaps he was faltering and needed this timely word of admonition.

Paul now ends his dictation of the letter to his scribe, takes up a quill, and straining through his dim, squinty eyes pens his personal greeting, the unmistakable seal of authenticity. He puts down his quill, seals the scroll, and hands it to Epaphras for delivery to Colossae.

SUMMARY

Now, we too are finished with the letter. But, having discovered its treasures we'll return to it again and again in the days and years ahead.

When I'm tempted to avoid the way of suffering required for ministry to others or faithfulness to Christ, I need to open the letter and see Paul's example of voluntary self-sacrifice, and hear again his ringing affirmation of suffering as ministry.

When relationships sour or I become careless in sustaining them I turn again to the letter, and I'm reminded of the high priority in which open, caring relationships must be held.

When I feel the pressures upon me to become preoccupied with the outward show of religiosity through mere conformity to rules and regulations, I do well to find again in the letter Paul's emphatic declaration that life in Christ is freedom, not bondage.

And when my vision dims and my courage falters, I can do no better than open the letter once more to be renewed and refreshed by the Apostle's masterful portrait of our risen and majestic Christ—the Lord of life and the Lord of the universe!

POINTS TO PONDER

1.   How do you respond to the statement: "Christianity is personal but it is not private?"

2.   Do you agree that husbands and wives are to be subject to each other? List some ways in which wives should be subject to their husbands. List some ways in which husbands should be subject to their wives.

3.   How do you see yourself as a parent? To what extent are you authoritarian? Permissive? Authoritative? How do you see your spouse?

4. Can you think of any things that you could initiate that might change the basic climate between you and your managers or employees?

5. Can you identify some friendships in your life that you initiated? Can you think of some that you could?

6. Is there some broken relationship in your life that you should seek to restore? What are you willing to do and when?